Alvis Saracen Family

ALVIS SARACEN FAMILY

Bill Munro

The Crowood Press

First published in 2002 by
The Crowood Press Ltd
Ramsbury, Marlborough
Wiltshire SN8 2HR

www.crowood.com

British Library Cataloguing-in-Publication Data
A catalogue record for this book is available from the British Library.

ISBN 1 86126 537 9

Acknowledgements
No historic vehicle book can be compiled without seeking help from other historians and, most importantly, the people who made them and used them. I am very grateful to all those listed below who gave of their time. If I have forgotten anyone, please forgive me.
Alvis staff, past and present: Roland Andrews MBE, Mike Dunn, Mike Harrow, Jim Kimberley, Alistair F. Phillips, Tom Packham, Alan Russell, Ted Smith, Val Thomas, Nicky Turner, Ron Walton.
From the Alvis Owner Club: Mark Chapman, Colin Smy, Eddie Tozeland, Guy Gregson, Anthony Kendrick, Terry Welsh.
Ex-RAF: John Arthur, John Cooper, Alistair Currah, Terry Harvey, Nigel Sheldon.
Ex-RCAF: Paul Landry, Ian Morrison, Don Teed and Joe Walker of firehouse651.com.
Ex-REME: Steve Gray, Graham Howland, Trevor Piper, M. J. Tanner.
Museums: David Fletcher and Martin Wickham, Tank Museum, Bovington; Royal Air Force Museum, Hendon; Barry Collins, Museum of British Road Transport, Coventry; Brian Baxter, Charles Elsey, Derek Gilliam and Roger Jones, REME Museum, Arborfield; Brian Harris and Steven Shirley, RAF Fire Museum, Manston.
Fellow writers and historians: Ken Day, Michael Eyre of the Crossley Register; Simon Rowley and John Shakespeare of the Fire Brigades Society: Geoff Fletcher, Pal Negyesi, Nick Walker, Pat Ware. Also: Bran Dragovitch, Melvyn Hiscock, Dale Johnson, Jim Thomas (retired) of AP Lockheed.
The author is especially grateful to Roland Andrews MBE, retired Superintendent, Wheeled Vehicle Division, Alvis for his invaluable help in producing the section 'Building a 600' and to John Rue for graciously allowing the use of notes he gathered for his book *Stout, Strong and Sturdy*.

Typeset by NBS Publications, Basingstoke, England

Printed and bound in Europe by Newton Printing Ltd. www.newtonprinting.com

Contents

1 'The Alvis'

The Second World War had taught the victorious armies many hard lessons. The British Army was seriously under-equipped in 1939 and a large proportion of our army's vehicles had been left in France in the retreat that culminated in the miracle of Dunkirk. British manufacturers worked flat out to produce as many new vehicles of all types as they possibly could, but it was thanks to Lend-Lease, through which a massive quantity of hardware was obtained from the USA, that the Allies could mount invasions of North Africa, Sicily and Normandy.

The motor vehicles used by the British Army were either of domestic, American or Canadian manufacture but, even where manufacturers like Ford or General Motors had plants in all three countries, there was a marked lack of standardization because there were many more makers than these. This was in many ways inevitable. Armies had mechanized to a degree in the Great War, but then horses were still widely used to draw artillery and supply vehicles and, until the Armistice, cavalry were waiting behind the lines to make the final breakthrough expected before Christmas 1914.

Pre-war military thinking prevailed throughout the 1920s and very little of what had been learned was put into practice. The US government would not spend any money and the British government had little money to spend. When the British Expeditionary Force set out for France in 1939 their vehicles were not generally of a standardized type and in 1944, when the Allies put together the massive invasion forces, the enormous numbers of vehicles used were sourced from wherever they could be found. Certainly there was standardization in the weights of truck specified, but the trucks themselves came from a wide number of manufacturers.

It would take a concerted effort from the designers to effect any form of standardization of military vehicles, but after the Second World War this was precisely the direction that the Ministry of Supply would take. As far as the manufacture of a new range of six-wheeled armoured fighting vehicles was concerned they would also chose a single company – Alvis of Coventry.

THE NAME 'ALVIS'

Much speculation has been passed about the meaning of the name Alvis. Is it Greek, Latin, Dutch or what? But when engineer Thomas George John began a new venture in 1919, he could have had no idea that this name would be the one under which the products of his company would gain worldwide respect.

Born in 1880, the son of a worker in Wales's Pembroke Dock, John was apprenticed in docks and, through a scholarship at the Royal College of Science, qualified as a naval architect in 1904. After a time at HM Dockyard in Devonport, where he became assistant constructor, John moved to the Coventry car-maker Siddeley-Deasy in 1915 as works manager. Here, as part of the company's war work, he worked on aero engines, particularly the Siddeley Puma, a derivative of the Beardmore-Halford-Pullinger (BHP) unit.

The well-known picture of Alvis's founder, T.G. John, at his desk. (MBRT, Coventry)

Many of the early influences on the British motor industry were from France and Germany. As a scholar of both the French and German languages, Kent-born Geoffrey P.H. de Freville was an ideal person to negotiate with continental manufacturers when he joined the Long Acre Car Company in 1902. In 1906 he became the manager of the British agency for the French firm of D. F. P., who were one of the first manufacturers to use aluminium pistons. In 1914, realizing the value of these items, de Freville formed Aluminium Alloy Pistons Ltd in Wandsworth, southwest London. He made these components for aircraft engines, where the power to weight ratio was so vital in early planes. In doing so, he made up the trade name 'Alvis' for them. And the name was nothing more than that – an invention.

T.G. John took his first step into business when, on 13 March 1919, he bought Holley Brothers Engineering in Hertford St, Coventry, and immediately changed the company's name to T.G. John & Co. Ltd. John's first catalogue advertised that he had the rights to sell Hillman cars and Electra stationary engines. He also built one of the first motor scooters, the Stafford Mobile Pup, on behalf of its designers, Stafford Auto Scooters Ltd of Coventry.

MOTOR CARS AND A CHANGE OF NAME

Geoffrey de Freville continued to be busy on his own account. He had designed a small, advanced, 1.5 litre four-cylinder sidevalve car engine using aluminium alloy pistons and pressure lubrication. No doubt having met, or at least heard about T.G. John through their mutual involvement in the aero engine business, de Freville approached him with ideas to manufacture his new engine. In consequence, John made an agreement with de Freville to build his new car on a royalty basis and, soon, to use the 'Alvis' name.

The first Alvis car, the 10/30, was introduced at the Scottish Motor Show in 1920 and went on sale the following July. At £750 with a basic two-seat body, it was expensive, but its top speed of 60mph (96km/h) was far better than average for its time. Looking soon for bigger premises, John acquired a machine shop in Holyhead Road, on the northwest side of Coventry, along the eastern side of the Coventry–Nuneaton railway line. Land behind the factory would enable further expansion. On 14 December 1920, John changed the name of the company again, to the Alvis Car and Engineering Company Ltd.

John's new company survived the economic slump of 1921–22. He introduced the improved 11/40 in 1922, which itself was replaced quickly by the 12/40, and the public bought some 700 of these cars. This year, the best yet, was also significant because two men who were to play a very important part in the Alvis history joined the company. Geoffrey de Freville's work at his Aluminium Piston Company had put him in touch with Captain George Thomas Smith-Clarke at the War Department's Aeronautical Inspection Directorate in Coventry. A Worcestershire man, Smith-Clarke's background was as a draughtsman with the Great Western Railway's Road Motor Department. Smith-Clarke joined Alvis as a senior engineer.

The second man was W. M. 'Willie' Dunn. A Scot, Dunn served an apprenticeship with J. Milburn Ltd, who were iron founders and engineers in Workington. He moved to Coventry to work as a draughtsman at Daimler and crossed to the south side of Holyhead Road to become chief draughtsman at Alvis.

The world of the motor car was where John and his company were firmly based at this time, and would be exclusively for the next eight years. The 10/30's performance had encouraged motor racing enthusiasts to race and tune it – an example with an overhead-valve engine won the Brooklands 200-mile race in 1923 – and encouraged by this, Smith-Clarke and Dunn began work on a Grand Prix car. Alvis were one of only two British makers to venture into this field, the other being Sunbeam, but for their GP car, Alvis's engineering brains were working on something revolutionary – front-wheel drive.

TROUBLED TIMES

Smith-Clarke and Dunn had already developed what would be considered as one of the finest light cars of its time, the legendary Alvis 12/50. Introduced in 1923, the 12/50's simple but well-engineered chassis and overhead-valve four-cylinder engine set the standard for many to follow. Unfortunately, Alvis was a victim of the 12/50's success, as orders far outstretched the undercapitalized company's finances. To help ease the financial situation, Henlys, Alvis's London dealers, often underwrote the company's debts, but a crisis came when, in 1924, Cross and Ellis, one of the suppliers of coachwork, sued for the £5,000 they were owed. Now Alvis were facing liquidation, but in 1925 they underwent major financial reconstruction, underpinned largely by a full order book for the 12/50. That year T.G. John, as a keen motor-racing enthusiast, authorized the building of the Grand Prix cars using a supercharged 1.5 litre straight-eight engine driving the front wheels.

By 1927 Alvis was growing steadily, selling 1,000 cars in that year. 1928 saw Alvis front-wheel-drive racing cars finish a remarkable sixth and ninth in the Le Mans 24-hour race. A front-wheel-drive production car, the 12/75, was introduced in 1928, but John was prudent enough to continue building rear-wheel-drive models, the 12/50 and the new six-cylinder 14/75, alongside it. That year the company produced record profits of £32,000, thriving in what was a difficult time for the motor industry as a whole. The success was not maintained in 1929, the year of the Wall Street crash. Nor were customers prepared to buy the front-wheel-drive cars in sufficient numbers to justify its continuation and they were dropped.

The car that made Alvis's name, the 12/50, with all-weather tourer coachwork. (MBRT, Coventry)

An Alvis 12/75 front-wheel-drive sports car. (MBRT, Coventry)

This six-cylinder 3½ litre Speed 20 with sorts saloon coachwork is a typical example of the high-quality cars that Alvis were producing in the 1930s. (MBRT, Coventry)

NEW DIRECTIONS

When Charles Follett opened a car agency in London in 1930 he entered a dealership arrangement with Alvis. It was one of three significant moves that would affect Alvis over the coming decade. When the new Speed 20 model, a powerful and refined 2.5 litre car, came out in 1932, Follett steered Alvis into a higher sector of the market. He was in accord with T.G. John, who saw that big manufacturers like Morris, Austin, Ford and Vauxhall, Standard and the 'new boys', the Rootes Group, were producing cheaper, reliable cars in all sizes, and in many cases offering sporting bodies as an option, at a price that Alvis would not be able to match. John and Follett decided that Alvis should be in the specialized, luxury market. As an idea of the quality of the Speed 20, it is understood that Rolls-Royce examined a Speed 20, considering it to be the type of car they should produce under their newly acquired Bentley name.

The other two changes, arrived at much as a result of the shift in the motor car market, came when John decided he should look at other types of business. John's experience at Siddeley-Deasy and Smith-Clarke's work during the Great War made them aware of the great advances in civil aviation at that time, and he and his board decided to move into the aero engine business.

But this was an extremely difficult time for any business, let alone for a motor manufacturer in a high-priced sector of the market, to make such a bold change. It was to prove not only necessary, but also extremely far-sighted. Car orders had fallen in 1934 and Alvis were anxious to see what the reaction was to the models at the Motor Show at Olympia that coming October. A good level of orders was placed for the Speed 20, putting the car factory up to full capacity with overtime. However, car sales in general would decline as the decade progressed and the black thunderhead of war swelled high over Europe. John's decision to

'The Alvis'. The sign on the elegant new factory frontage says 'Aero engines' and 'Cars', dating this picture to the mid-1930s before fighting vehicles were even a part of Alvis's output. (Martin Wickham)

diversify was wise, although it would be some years before the seeds would grow, blossom and bear their best fruit.

Development work on the cars continued; after all, it was still Alvis's core business and they had already established a tradition of innovation. The growing number of women drivers were demanding a better gearbox than the common 'crash' type. The pre-selector gearbox was gaining favour in larger cars. In 1933–4 cars were offered with an ENV pre-selector box, but rather than use the fluid coupling pioneered by Daimler, which absorbed a not insignificant amount of power, Smith-Clarke experimented with a centrifugal clutch. Neither this nor the pre-selector box was a success in Alvis models. More significantly, Alvis took out a licence from General Motors in America to build an all-synchromesh gearbox. They constructed one to their own design within that licence and it proved very popular.

Experiments with rubber suspension also took up time, but these were abandoned as the components wore out too quickly. The front-wheel-drive cars had featured independent front-suspension, with four leading quarter-elliptical springs. The big Crested Eagle of 1934 was the first rear-wheel-drive Alvis to feature independent front-suspension, but this used a transverse leaf spring. The work in suspension and transmissions was possibly the most progressive by any UK vehicle manufacturer and gave Alvis a firm foundation for the work they were to do in years to come, especially in the field of armoured fighting vehicles.

The year of 1935 was an eventful one. Diversifying into a new line of business meant that the old company name would seem too restrictive to new customers, so it was changed once more, to

Alvis Ltd. In March, the chairman, Sir Arthur Lowes Dickinson, died. His place was taken by T.G. John, adding to his already heavy workload. By August, aero engine manufacture came much closer, when a £50,000 licence was taken out from the French company, the Société des Moteurs Gnome et Rhône. This company had built some of the best, most reliable rotary aero engines during the Great War. Work had begun on a new factory, which would cost them £87,000. Like the original car factory, this too was on Holyhead Road, but on the western side of the railway line. J. Pontremoli was appointed chief engineer of Aero engine plant. The future offered some promise of Air Ministry aero engine orders, but a drop in profits to £28,000, because of a slump in car sales, caused serious worry.

FIGHTING VEHICLES

But it was the threat of war that instigated the third of those crucial moves for Alvis, the most important for our story. The Great War had been called 'The War to End All Wars' and in its aftermath the 'Old Guard' at the War Office turned their backs on the great advances in technology: the development of the tank, the huge improvements in road transport and the revolution in air power. They regarded all of this as a passing phase, believing that the horse was still the real way to wage war. British armed forces were taken back at least ten years as the government, hard pressed to keep the economy stable and having very little money to spend on defence needs, allowed this retrograde and ultimately futile thinking to continue.

But events in the mid-1930s were to shake open those dreaming eyes, or to find the old men displaced by new, younger blood that recognized that the future of warfare was with mechanization. And war was spreading across the globe. Japan was building itself an empire in the Far East; Mussolini in Italy had the same idea and occupied the virtually defenceless countries of North Africa; Spain would be wracked by civil war; and Adolf Hitler marched his army into the Rhineland in direct contravention of the Treaty of Versailles. As some kind of answer to this, the British government begun a rearmament programme and, in 1934, foreseeing what would happen, John started negotiations with the War Office for work for the new Mechanizations Department he had set up.

Nicholas Straussler's Armoured Cars

The RAF had a tradition of using armoured cars, starting from the time when one of its constituent services, the Royal Naval Air Service, used Rolls-Royces and Napiers in France in the Great War. Britain had been given a mandate in 1919 to control the Arab nations following the break-up of the Ottoman Empire and in Mesopotamia the RAF used armoured cars to keep rebellious Arab factions under control.

The Army were testing a new type of armoured car for the RAF, designed by Hungarian Nicholas Straussler. The long-established Hungarian industrial concern Manfred Weiss had built a prototype in Budapest for Straussler, but when Hungary sided with the Nazis in the early 1930s, Straussler found himself in England, searching for a new manufacturer. He found it in Alvis. Straussler's armoured car was the first ever purpose-built type, rather than one converted from an existing car or lorry chassis. The Army's trials for the RAF included a drive from Port Said at the mouth of the Suez Canal across the desert to Baghdad, and tests in Palestine. It performed well. Straussler did not have the finance to put this vehicle into production and Alvis were quick to take advantage of the situation. In July 1936 an Alvis subsidiary, Alvis-Straussler Mechanization Ltd, was formed, with T.G. John as chairman and Willie Dunn as service manager and manager.

Alvis-Straussler ACII

The first Alvis-Straussler armoured car to enter production was the ACII. The backbone chassis was built by Manfred Weiss in Budapest, to the same design as the original Straussler prototype,

A Straussler armoured car, built by M. Weiss in Hungary, where it was photographed. (Tank Museum, Bovington)

The ACII on test in Scotland. The car behind is an Alvis saloon, possibly a Silver Eagle. (Tank Museum, Bovington)

An ACII on test in Palestine for the RAF. (Tank Museum, Bovington)

'And just for a prank, they sent us a tank that ties itself in knots!' Noël Coward's wonderful lyric from 'Could You Please Oblige Us With a Bren Gun?', a song that tells of the plight of an under-equipped Home Guard company, could have been written for the Alvis-Straussler light tank. Its tiller steering, which controlled the throttles of its two independent engines, was not liked by the Army. Here it is at Alvis's test ground at Baginton, to the southeast of Coventry. Its tracks were actually removable to allow it to run on metalled roads without causing damage. The tender vehicle is a Hefty gun tractor. (Tank Museum, Bovington)

and imported. It featured four-wheel drive and four-wheel steering and all-independent suspension using A-frames and single transverse leaf springs. It was adapted to take the latest and biggest 4.3 litre six-cylinder engine from the passenger car. The Alvis Straussler was designed to be driven from either end, and had steering gear with interchangeable ratios to suit either road or off-road use and servo-assisted Bendix brakes.

The armoured car was a successful design, with a total of twenty-four built. Orders were completed and exported to the Dutch East Indies and to Portugal, where they performed well. The Air Ministry ordered eleven, and interest was shown from India.

The Straussler Light Tank

Straussler also designed a light tank, and Alvis-Straussler built prototypes for this with the intention of putting it into production. It was tiny as tanks go, just 15ft 6in (4.72m) long and weighing in at 8.4 tons (8,550kg). Its power was from two 4.3 litre Alvis engines, and its armour was 0.6in (14mm) thick. The War Office ordered two for tests, but severe shortcomings were found. Its hard ride proved too uncomfortable for the crew and gradient tests resulted in the tracks coming adrift. The steering was by joystick and the army testers found this unsatisfactory, as it was a totally different system to the one used on other tanks. Its only real virtue was a top speed of 40mph (64km/h). The War Department rejected it.

Other countries expressed an interest in the tank. One order came from Russia, another from Poland and two from Holland. Apart from the two delivered to the War Department, only Poland received a tank, which it refused to accept. The Alvis-Straussler light tank was doomed to failure.

The Hefty

By now the government's re-armament programme was well under way, and much work was put out for tender. The principle of the backbone chassis that had shown itself to be successful on the ACII armoured car was used for the Hefty gun tractor. Rather than use their own 4.3 litre OHV six, which had worked well in the armoured car, Alvis chose to equip the Hefty with a 3.6 litre sidevalve Ford V8. This was a tough, well-proven and easily maintained engine, already in use in Army vehicles. Four-wheel drive was fitted, being mandatory for the type of vehicle. Weighing between 4–5 tons, it could tow an 8 ton load. Apart from some interest shown by Belgium, the Hefty was abandoned and more conventional gun tractors from Morris and Ford eventually adopted.

The LAC

In 1938 Nicholas Straussler resigned from Alvis-Straussler Ltd and the company was reformed as Alvis Mechanization Ltd. Building on its experience with the Straussler vehicles and its own work with transmissions and suspension, the new company concentrated on producing its own designs for fighting vehicles. The first vehicle produced by the new company was the LAC. This was Alvis Mechanization's answer to a requirement for a light armoured vehicle to be built from proprietary auto parts. Alvis equipped the LAC with two Ford V8 engines. One engine drove the left-hand wheels, the other the right-hand, each with its own gearbox, but there was a connected throttle and gear change. Its driveline was the most interesting, with the drive from each transmission being connected directly to the hubs, with no axles. Transverse leaf springs provided full independent suspension. The development of this vehicle was halted by the outbreak of war, when more conventional vehicles were purchased.

The Alvis Dingo

The last fighting vehicle to be developed by Alvis before the outbreak of war was the Dingo. A scout car, it was somewhat similar in type to the

Daimler's light armoured car, given the name Dingo in place of the Alvis. The drivetrain of the Dingo was very close in pattern to its bigger brothers, the Daimler scout car and armoured car. The Eighth Army 'Desert Rat' markings show the specific interest of this preserved vehicle's owner. (Bill Munro)

Straussler armoured car and the LAC in that it had a tubular backbone chassis and transverse-leaf all-independent suspension. Power came from the four-cylinder 12/70 car engine. Like the Straussler tank it was fast, being capable of 55mph (88km/h), but the engine wore badly in service and it was less stable off-road than its heavier, more powerful competitor from Daimler. Again, war stopped the development of the Alvis and the name Dingo was taken for the Daimler.

The Daimler Dingo

Daimler's Dingo was a startlingly new design in itself. Designed from scratch in 1938 by a team of engineers under Sid Shellard, the Dingo had a six-cylinder 2.5 litre ohv rear-mounted engine and a welded all-steel hull. But the most interesting part of it was the drivetrain. The centrally mounted differential was coupled to a five-speed Daimler pre-selector gearbox. From the differential, longitudinal driveshafts ran forward and aft to bevel boxes at each wheel. Short driveshafts with Tracta joints took the drive from box to wheel. The driveline pattern was adopted for the larger Daimler armoured car, which differed from the Dingo only in its size, with a 3.8 litre engine and reduction gears in the hubs to enable the extra torque of the engine to cope with the vehicle's weight.

AERO ENGINE PROGRESS

A new airport for Coventry had been built at Baginton, to the southeast of the city. In 1936 Alvis bought land adjacent to it, where they built an aero engine test house. By September the new factory was finished, but they hadn't any work for it, as no orders for the aero engine were in the offing. Work had to be sourced elsewhere and firms who already were supplying the government were contacted to see if they had anything to sub-contract out.

The search for work for the aero engine factory resulted in some subcontract work for Rolls-Royce and 1,000 airscrews were made for the De Havilland aircraft company. The very first Alvis aero engine, the 1,100bhp Pelides fourteen-cylinder radial, completed its test run 15 March 1937. Interest in it came from three aircraft manufacturers – Fairey, Scottish Aviation and Vickers – but the lack of firm aero-engine orders, the decline in car sales and problems in construction of armoured cars resulted in a trading loss for the end of July 1937 of £30,000. After the successful running of the Pelides, the works manager, J. Pontremoli, demanded a higher salary. When this was refused, he resigned. George H. Lanchester was then recruited as manager of the mechanization department. He envisaged the production of smaller aero engines to an exclusive Alvis design.

Although tests proved the Pelides satisfactory, the British government declared that it would not order any aero engines based on a French design. Its decision stemmed from an argument over a Gnome design from 1914. The Air Ministry placed a development order for the new Leonides engine, a design of Alvis's own, which was a great help for the company. However, the sheer pressure of work had an adverse effect on T.G. John and he was forced into semi-retirement.

BUSY BUT UNCERTAIN TIMES

Subcontract work for Rolls-Royce and De Havilland kept the factory fully occupied, but the company lost £78,000 in the year to mid-1938. After placing the development orders for the Leonides aero engine, the government expressed concern that the aero engine factory was not being used for its intended purpose. The Leonides had proved itself a very good engine in flight tests, with General Aircraft and Fokker expressing an interest in it. Some income came from letting out the Baginton test facilities to the Royal Navy, and the Cierva and Hafner companies, both helicopter and autogyro pioneers, showed an interest in the Leonides. The car plant was running at half capacity, but experiments with hydraulic suspension on the Speed 20 and with rubber and coil springs on the Silver Crest were undertaken to try to further improve the ride and handling.

WAR

At the outbreak of the Second World War in September 1939, Alvis was in profit, although the aero engine factory had yet to build a single engine for sale and the car plant was running at half capacity. As far as the armoured car was concerned, the Belgian government showed interest in it and there were talks with the Turkish government. The Rumanians actually ordered fifty, but the war put an end to all deals.

Much of Alvis's profit was in subcontracting for other aero engine manufacturers and it was this type of work that Alvis was engaged on throughout the war. Alvis, with its record of engineering excellence, provided a very useful and skilled contribution to the war effort. Most of this was aero engine work; assembling Rolls-Royce Kestrel, Merlin and Griffon engines, component manufacture for and overhaul and repair of these and of American engines. Construction of aircraft bomb trolleys and overhaul of RAF ground equipment were two jobs carried out at any one the eleven satellite factories Alvis now controlled.

The horrific Luftwaffe raid on Coventry on the night of 14 November 1940 saw the car plant heavily damaged. The aero engine plant on the other side of the railway line received damage too and there was loss of life as neighbouring homes were bombed. Much of Alvis's war work was disseminated to factories at Stone in Staffordshire, Leicester, Berkshire and Middlesex, both to increase capacity and to minimize the effects of the bombing. In another raid the following April the main tool room was destroyed, emphasizing the company's wisdom in deciding to spread the work out.

T.G. JOHN STEPS DOWN

Devotion of one's life to a new, progressive company, particularly when taking it through severe economic times, and having the courage to branch out into fields already occupied by established competitors can be extremely demanding on any individual. So it was with T.G. John. He had already gone into semi-retirement and in 1943 his doctor ordered total rest. By the following year his health had deteriorated to such an extent that he had to retire completely. He surely would have been cheered by the news in 1943 when the government placed firm orders for the Leonides aero engine. One of his two dreams for the future was beginning to come true. The other, the successful production of fighting vehicles, would materialize soon.

War work was profitable and enabled Alvis to pay off the debts it had incurred in the aero engine development programme. Alvis could look forward to peacetime business with some degree of optimism.

2 A New Generation of Fighting Vehicles

Alvis Ltd resumed peacetime work with every intent of following the same strategy as T.G. John had started in the mid-1930s. There would be three main lines of business: cars, aero engines and military contracts for the Ministry of Supply. Following T.G. John's retirement in 1944, the Alvis board had already spoken to the man they wanted as the new managing director. He was J.J. Parkes, who joined them on 1 January 1946 from the engine and propeller division of De Havilland Aircraft, a company that had supplied Alvis with much subcontract work. Parkes, described by those who worked with him as a true gentleman, had a reputation for being good at cutting out waste, a useful talent in any business but especially so in the difficult climate of the mid-1940s. However, a sad note marked the end of the old era. T.G. John had been living in retirement Putney, southwest London, and the whole of Alvis was in mourning when they learned of his death in August 1946. He was just sixty-six.

J.J. Parkes, managing director and later chairman of Alvis Ltd. (MBRT, Coventry)

John Parkes' contacts in the aircraft industry were no doubt extremely useful. Much of the work put into the Leonides aero engine started to fulfil its designers' intentions in 1946 when a total of fifty were ordered by Cunliffe-Owen Ltd, Westland, Fairey and Bristol. Early the following year the Air Ministry asked Alvis to tender for a flat 450bhp engine for helicopter use, which resulted in the development and production of the fourteen-cylinder Leonides Major radial. With raw materials scarce, especially steel, supplies could best be obtained if the company took a government order, so Alvis began to make aircraft carrier bomb-trolleys for the Admiralty. The government, via the Ministry of Supply, was also the source of a contract to make printing machines. This was somewhat unusual work considering the company's past products. Still, they had been founded as an engineering company and had accumulated considerable expertise. The contract would be a valuable source of income and retained a number of skilled men within the company.

(Left) *The Alvis Leonides aero engine. This nine-cylinder radial had an excellent reputation for reliability. (MBRT, Coventry)*

(Below) *The Thompson-British Automatic Platen Printing Press, as built by Alvis. (MBRT, Coventry)*

NEW CARS

Development work on new cars, begun in the last months of the war, continued. There would be, it was envisaged, two lines: a smaller car, based around the pre-war 12/70 and called the TA14; and a 3 litre, with a modern saloon bodyshell and an all-new six-cylinder engine. However, the severe shortage of steel caused the government to ration its allocation. Car companies would receive favourable quantities if they could produce large numbers of vehicles for export. Alvis was a small-scale car producer – Rolls-Royce had made more cars in the 1930s than Alvis – and with such limited export potential qualified for very little steel. Besides, Alvis had never made bodies for their own cars, preferring to subcontract this out to the coachbuilding trade. Now this side of the motor industry had been cut back to a fraction of its former size by the rise of the pressed-steel body, the drop in the market for high-quality cars and the dire shortage of craftsmen. To have a pressed-steel body for the 3 litre they would have to pay a company like Pressed Steel Bodies for expensive press tools; this would be far too expensive for a car that was to be produced in modest numbers, so the concept was soon revised. An enlarged version of the TA14, the TA21, would have to fit the bill, sharing the same style of coachbuilt saloon body by Mulliners of Birmingham as its smaller brother. Drophead coupés would be offered on both chassis, a choice of a budget-priced pressed-steel version by Carbodies or a more expensive timber-framed body by Tickford on the TA14 and by Tickford alone on the TA21.

An Alvis TA14 drophead coupé. This example has coachwork by Carbodies, who were opposite Alvis on Holyhead Road. (Bill Munro)

FIGHTING VEHICLES

But compared to its pre-war importance, car production would play an ever-decreasing role in Alvis's output. Fighting vehicles would begin to assume a significant role. Before the war, these had been produced by the subsidiary company Alvis Mechanization Ltd. This was now renamed the Wheeled Vehicle Division, with Captain Smith-Clarke as its senior engineer and Willie Dunn as his assistant. As a result of the involvement with Nicholas Straussler, all Alvis fighting-vehicle drawings would be prefixed with the letters AS and all fighting vehicles would have names that began with the letter 'S'.

Following the Second World War, the Department of Tank Design (DTD) started a design for a range of six-wheeled high-mobility vehicles, to be capable of operating in extremes of conditions across the world. The six-wheel configuration decided upon by the DTD was at the time thought to be the optimum arrangement for cross-country work. British armoured cars in service at the time were of four-wheeled design, but the American six-wheeled M8 and captured examples of the German eight-wheeled SdKfz 234 vehicles gave the opportunity to assess different configurations. For the design engineers it was a matter of getting

Among the aircraft types using the Alvis Leonides was the Percival Provost trainer for the Royal Air Force. The engines had an excellent reputation for smooth running and reliability. This example is maintained in flying condition by is owner, Alan House. (Melvyn Hiscock)

the right balance between weight, performance, serviceability, shipping capability and production costs. Four-wheeled vehicles had been seen to encounter difficulties in crossing ditches or cresting knife-edge ridges, whereas a central pair of wheels would enable the vehicle to keep drive on the ground at all times. Eight-wheeled vehicles, whilst capable of carrying a greater weight of arms, armour and crew, were much more complex and heavy, more expensive to produce, less agile in the reconnaissance role as operated by the British Army and they took up more space in transport ships and aircraft.

Truck or heavy motor car chassis had been used by some countries as the basis for early armoured cars, but Daimler armoured cars were designed and built with an all-steel welded hull of, to borrow a phrase that would be used by the car industry in the future, unit construction. As a new type of vehicle construction, problems were to be expected. Naturally the steel used had to be tough enough to make a strong box for the vehicle and also be sufficiently resistant to shells. Manual arc welding was introduced on ferrous armour plate around the beginning of the war and some cracking problems were experienced in the welds due to the high carbon content of the steel. A Ministry of Defence directive limited the carbon content to 0.32 carbon in the manufacture of ferrous armour plate, which permitted satisfactory welding to be carried out to produce a strong vehicle that retained an adequate ballistic performance. Britain was the only country to take this step. Examination of German and Russian equipment revealed substantial weld cracking. Perhaps they had traded off weldability and structural integrity for higher ballistic performance.

STANDARDIZATION

With the pressure of war now gone the standardization of types and components in as many military vehicles as possible could now be put into practice. This is precisely what the Ministry of Supply, the government body responsible for procuring equipment for the British Armed Forces, would do. Following a visit by representatives of the Army Mechanization Board in the spring of 1947, Alvis were requested to undertake the design of a new fighting vehicle, coded FV600. Some debate had been undertaken about the nature of this vehicle. The size and type of tank in use was under review, and the light tank was facing obsolescence. Some members of the Royal Armoured Corps were not happy about this. They considered the light tank to be an important vehicle for reconnaissance and for support of the flanks of advancing infantry. However, the decision for an armoured reconnaissance vehicle fell in favour of a wheeled vehicle, an armoured car. It was numbered FV601 and named Saladin after the twelfth-century Sultan who fought against the Crusades. It was envisaged that it would weigh around 10 tons, fitting in size in between the Daimler and Greyhound armoured cars, at around 7½ tons each, and the Coventry (11 tons), the AEC (12½ tons) and the Deerhound (13 tons). After building a one-eighth scale model, Alvis would be required to produce one prototype for British evaluation, and possibly a second prototype for the US government.

A great deal of work had gone into the design of the suspension, particularly in the study of American wheeled armoured cars. The 6×6 Chevrolet T19, too heavy a design to go into production, had all-independent suspension. The M8, made by then in considerable numbers by the Ford Motor Company in the USA and known to the British as the Greyhound, was also a 6×6, but in typical Ford fashion it had live axles on leaf springs. Its proposed replacement, the T28, had independent suspension with double A-frames, the design of which was adopted by the newly formed FVDD for the new British fighting vehicle series. The driveline for the new series was based on that designed by Daimler for the Dingo and Armoured Car. This consisted of a centrally mounted transmission,

The Rolls-Royce B-Series Engines

The sudden growth in the size of the armed forces during the Second World War demanded that not only British but also American and Canadian motor manufacturers produced a huge range of vehicles. The short notice of this meant that the Allies had to take what was available at the time, with comparatively little opportunity to effect any standardization. So allied forces went into battle at first with a mixture of vehicles, powered by an equally diverse variety of powerplants. Not only that, but there were two different standards of threads; domestic British vehicles such as Austin, Morris, Standard, Hillman and Morris were using British standard (BSF) thread sizes, whilst the American-owned British manufacturers, Ford and Bedford, and the Americans themselves – Chevrolet, Dodge, Studebaker, Willys-Overland and so on – used the Society of Automotive Engineers' Unified (UNF/UNC) threads. This demanded two complete sets of spanners and two separate lots of nuts and bolts in every workshop.

Before the end of the war, development began of standard ranges of military vehicles and a range of petrol engines to power them, of various capacities and different numbers of cylinders. These would have to be durable, easily serviceable and use as many standardized components as possible.

Rolls-Royce had a long connection with the military. The Hawk and Eagle aero engines saw service in the Great War, as did Rolls-Royce Silver Ghost armoured cars. TheV12 Merlin was the most famous aero engine of this lineage, powering the Hurricane and Spitfire fighters and the Lancaster bomber. It was the basis of the Meteor, used in the Cromwell and Centurion tanks. With such a pedigree, Rolls-Royce was chosen to build the new series of military engines, which were based on the new power plant for the post-war passenger cars.

The range would have a 'signature' stroke of 4½in (114.3mm) and a standard bore of 3½in (89mm). There would be the four-cylinder B40, of 2.8 litres, the six-cylinder B60 of 4.25 litres and the straight-eight, 5.675 litre B80. For the most demanding of applications a 6.5 litre B81 was developed with the 3¾in (95.5mm) bore it would share with the later six-cylinder Rolls-Royce and Bentley passenger car engine. All had monobloc cast-iron cylinders with integral crank case. The detachable cylinder head, aluminium in some early B80s but otherwise cast iron, housed the inlet valves, whilst the exhaust valves were in the cylinder block. This F-head design allowed for much larger inlet valves and thus better breathing, whilst making for quiet running. The compression ratio was kept low so as to allow the vehicles to run on poor-grade petrol. The engines were designed to be operated at extremes of climate, from −40 to 120°F (−40 to 49°C) to cope with any environment the armed forces might find themselves in. Both wet- and dry-sump versions would be made to allow for as many different applications as possible.

The new engines were available from 1948, in good time for the Saladin. The very early engines in the series used the BSF threads that Rolls-Royce had been using since they first started making motor cars, but soon switched over to UNF – engines built with this thread had 'UNF' stamped on the rocker cover.

Typical Installations

The 80bhp B40 was the engine of the new Austin Champ, the vehicle that would replace the Willys MB/Ford GPW jeep then in service with the British Army. The Champ proved too expensive to buy. A small number of Series I Land Rovers were fitted with B40 engines in place of the then standard 1.5 litre F-head unit – the intent was to produce a cheaper quarter-ton vehicle with a standardized power unit. This experiment was not successful but the later Series II Land Rover with its own new 2.2 litre petrol engine eventually replaced the Champ.

The 130bhp B60 was fitted to the Ferret and Fox scout cars, the Humber FV1609 one-ton truck and its armoured variants, and in some Dennis fire engines. The B80 engine was used in the Saracen, Saladin and the Thornycroft Mk5 fire crash tender. The B81 was installed in the Leyland Martian heavy artillery tractor, the Thornycroft Mk7 fire crash tender, the Salamander and the Stalwart.

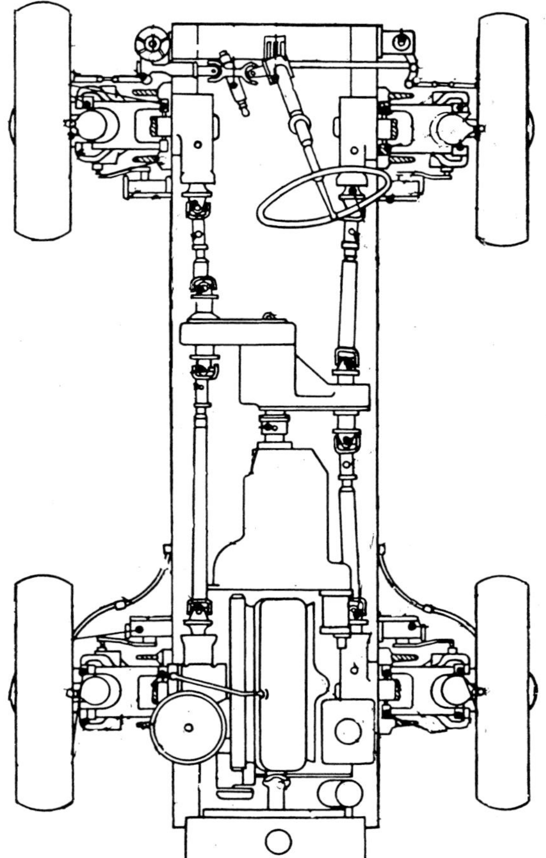

The driveline layout of the Daimler scout car with its rear-mounted engine, coupled via a pre-selector gearbox to a transfer box. The driveshafts take the drive to the front and rear wheels, and bevel boxes take the drive through right angles to the wheels. This layout would be the basis of the FV600 series. (REME Museum)

with longitudinal driveshafts taking the drive to bevel boxes at each wheel station and short driveshafts with Tracta joints taking the drive to the wheels.

From the Fighting Vehicle Research Establishment (FVRDE) Alvis received the specification of the armoured car. Along with it came the definition of its role, which was:

- Ground reconnaissance with the infantry
- Pursuit and harassing of retreating armoured formation
- Effective engagement of infantry and unarmoured vehicles and weapons, comparable enemy vehicles at short range caught at a disadvantage
- Protection such as to give greatest possible immunity to attack by ½in (1.27cm) SAAP at a range of 300yd (275m) over a frontal arc of 45 degrees and complete protection to crew and internal components against:
    - Attack from 7.92mm SAAP from any direction
    - The equivalent 25pdr shell splinters

from a ground burst 30ft (9m) from the vehicle

- The detonation under any wheel of either a mine containing 20lb (9kg) explosive or a mine that will not overturn the vehicle.

The specification stated:

- An all-steel hull, welded at all joints and sealed against the ingress of water
- The main power unit to be the Rolls-Royce B80 straight-eight water-cooled petrol engine, driving through a five-speed semi-automatic transmission and a forward-and-reverse single range transfer box
- Suspension to be all-independent by wishbone sprung either by torsion bar or coil springs
- The vehicle should be capable of being steered from either the front or rear end, and be by recirculating ball. The steering wheel for the front of the vehicle should be approximately parallel to the glacis plate, and vertical at the rear
- Require armour for immunity to near misses from medium artillery, including air bursts or from a 20lb mine
- The primary armament to be a 2pdr Pipsqueak HV gun and coaxially mounted machine gun
- The vehicle would be required to carry a crew of four: a commander, a driver, a gunner and a loader
- The maximum gross weight of the vehicle, including W/T set, twenty-seven rounds of ammunition, drinking water and lashing gear for airborne operations was to be 10 tons

The Saladin wooden mock-up, front view. The small bore of the two-pounder Pipsqueak gun is evident, even as a dummy. (Tank Museum, Bovington)

The rear view of the Saladin wooden mock-up. The cylindrical device attached to the rear wing is the silencer. (Tank Museum, Bovington)

- The overall dimensions should not exceed: 7ft 4in (2.23m) height over cupola, 6ft 11in (2.11m) over the top of the turret, 5ft (1.52m) to the top of the hull, 16ft 2in (4.93m) overall length, 17ft 9in (5.41m) length over the gun barrel, 8ft 5in (2.57m) overall width, 6ft 8in (2.03m) maximum track, 10ft (3.05m) wheelbase, 1ft 4in (0.41m) minimum ground clearance, approach angle of 60 degrees front and 50 degrees rear, a maximum road speed of 50mph (80km/h), a maximum safe road speed of 35mph (56km/h) and a maximum speed in reverse of 20mph (32km/h)
- The vehicle should have standard WD pattern wheels with non-skid chains to be fitted as required
- Brakes were specified as drums all round
- Two jettisonable escape doors should be provided each side of the vehicle. The loader would have his own periscope and escape hatch separate from that of the commander
- The gun should elevate to a maximum of 25 degrees and be depressed a maximum of 12 degrees, including to the rear of the vehicle.
- Armour thickness would be 8mm on the front visor, 10mm on the scuttle, 8mm on the glacis plate, 10mm on the skid plate and 12mm on the side plate.

The specification required first a wooden mock-up, which had been produced, and subsequently a prototype to designs produced by the renamed Fighting Vehicle Research and Development Establishment (FVRDE).

Saladin Mk1 – FVRDE Specification

Role	Armoured Reconnaissance Car
Engine	
Type	One Rolls-Royce B80 Mk3A in-line eight-cylinder petrol engine; monobloc cast-iron construction; inlet-over-exhaust valves; detachable aluminium cylinder-head; dry-sump lubrication
Capacity	5,760cc
Bore	3$^{1}/_{2}$in (88.9mm)
Stroke	4$^{1}/_{2}$in (114.29mm)
Compression ratio	6.4:1
Power	160bhp at 3,750rpm
Torque	261lb/ft at 2,300rpm
Governed speed	3,750rpm
Ignition type	Coil, 24v
Transmission	
Gearbox	Five-speed pre-selector, fluid coupling
Transfer box	Forward and reverse, single range, giving five forward and five reverse speeds
Differential	Single, centrally mounted
Propeller shafts	Muff coupling
Axles	Articulating shafts with two Tracta joints per shaft
Hub gearing	4.125:1 double epicyclic
Brakes	
Foot	Hydraulic, drums on all wheels, hydraulic servo
Hand	Mechanical on all wheels
Steering	
System	Recirculating ball, divided, acting on front and centre wheels
Servo mechanism	Hydraulic
Suspension	Independent on all six wheels, with unequal length wishbones and longitudinal torsion bars with sleeves giving 10in total travel. Damping by two telescopic shock absorbers and two rebound dampers per road wheel.
Wheels and Tyres	
Wheels	10.00 × 20 WD pattern divided disc
Tyres	11.00 × 20 Run flat
Dimensions	
Length	(Vehicle over gun barrel) 16ft 4in (5m)
Height to turret	6ft 11in (1.9m)
Height to cupola	6ft 6in (2m)
Width overall	8ft 3in (2.5m)
Track	6ft 8in (2.1m)
Wheelbase	10ft (3m) overall (5ft, 5ft) between axles
Ground clearance, unladen	1ft 5in (0.4m)
Angle of approach	50 degrees (889 mils)
Turning circle	45ft (13.7m)
Gross weight	22,400lb (10,150kg)
Crew	Four – driver, commander, gunner and loader
Electrical Equipment	24v negative earth system
Armament	
Main turret	2pdr Pipsqueak gun, two .50 machine guns, one coaxial in turret, one on Commander's cupola

PROTOTYPES

The first running prototype was slightly smaller in some dimensions than the specified maximum, being shorter by 7in over the gun barrel, 1¼in shorter in hull length and 1in narrower. It was, however, 2in taller than specified, but an increase of 1in in ground clearance accounted for some of this.

The power train was wholly contained within the hull. The engine, a Rolls-Royce eight-cylinder B series as specified, was mounted between the rear wheels, as in the Dingo and larger Daimler armoured cars, in a fore-and-aft position on four mounting points with the radiator behind it. The engine drove through a fluid coupling to a Wilson pre-selector gearbox with five forward speeds. Attached in-unit to the gearbox, in the centre of the vehicle was a single-range transfer box and differential. This transfer box provided the required reversing facility, giving the gearbox five forward and five reverse speeds and turning the drive at right angles to the output shaft of the gearbox.

The drive was taken from either side of the transfer box, outwards to bevel boxes in line in a vertical plane with the central road wheels. From these, driveshafts mounted on the inside of each side of the hull ran fore and aft to more bevel boxes, one each in line with the front and rear road wheels. Attached to the bevel boxes were short driveshafts with a Tracta joint at each end, to take the drive to the road wheels. A planetary gear set in each wheel hub provided a final reduction gearing for the road wheels. The differential in the transfer box was the only one in the driveline, thus the only differential action was between the left- and right-hand side, but not between the centre and the front and rear wheels. The steering was on the front and centre

The FV601A Saladin prototype, weighted down to simulate the weight of ammunition and turret, on test at FVRDE Chertsey. (Tank Museum, Bovington)

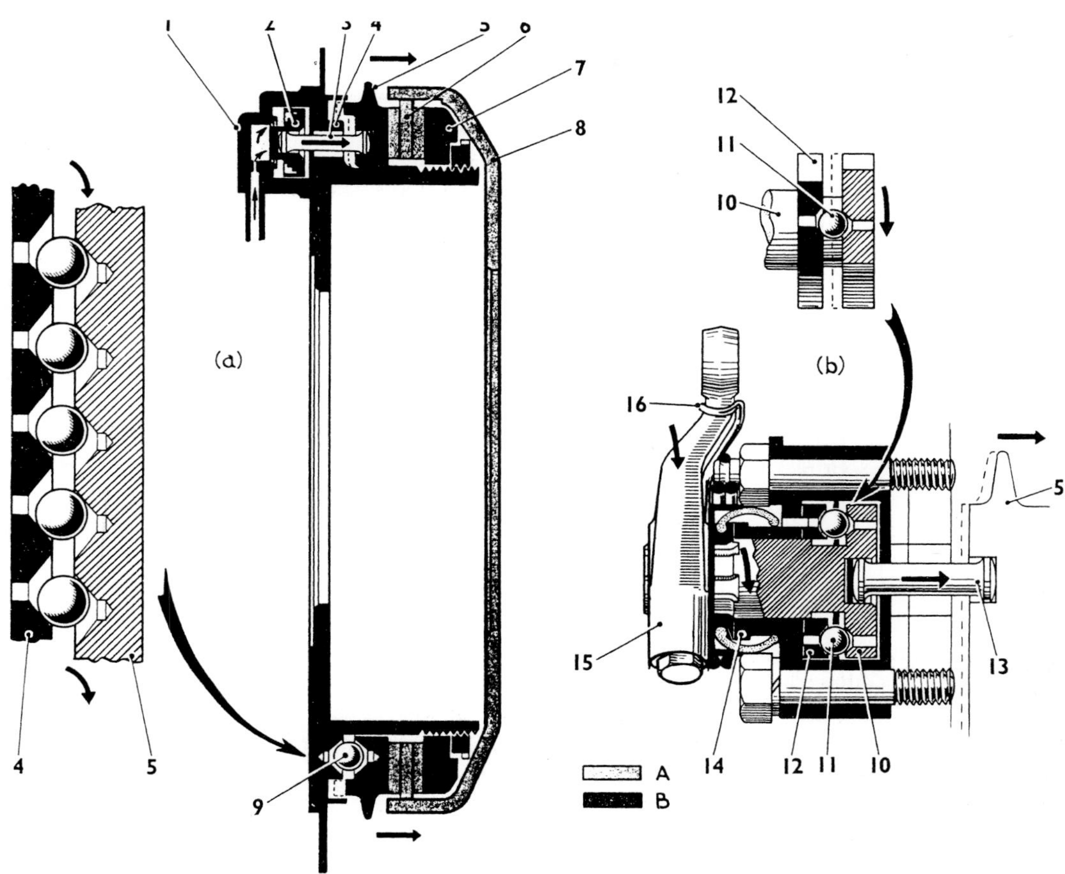

Saladin Ring Brake (REME Museum)

1 Wheel cylinder
2 Piston
3 Push rod
4 Backplate flange piece
5 Inner pressure plate
6 Friction lined centre plate
7 Outer pressure plate
8 Drum
9 Steel ball
10 Handbrake shaft
11 Steel ball
12 Handbrake housing washer
13 Pushrod
14 Handbrake housing
15 Handbrake shaft lever
16 Lever return spring
(a) Operation of footbrake
A Fluid pressure
B Revolving parts
(b) Operation of handbrake
The friction-lined centre plate (6) is attached to the drum (8) and rotates with it. When the brake is applied, the wheel cylinders press the inner and outer pressure plates (5 and 7 respectively) onto the rotating friction plate.

driving wheels, through a power-assisted recirculating-ball box as specified. Two driving positions were specified, an additional one at the rear.

The prototypes were to be tested, minus the gun, in line with FVRDE proving trials regulations. The reliability test was to be over a 10,000-mile period, with 50 per cent of the work cross-country and the other 50 per cent on hard roads. Reports were made at 2,500, 5,000 and 10,000 miles. The Saladin would be required to maintain an average speed of not less than 35mph over 25 miles during a 100-mile run, and reach its intended maximum speed of 50mph within a straight and level course of a quarter mile.

The 11ton laden weight of the Saladin and the speeds that it would be capable of created demands that the FVRDE felt current brake technology couldn't handle. Thus Borg and Beck Lockheed built a new type of ring brake to a design developed by the FVRDE in the late 1940s at Chertsey. At this time disc brakes were unheard of in production cars. Chrysler in America would offer them as an option in 1949, but it would not be until 1953 that a C-Type Jaguar fitted with what is now recognized as the conventional calliper-type disc brake would win the Le Mans 24-hour race. It would be a further six years before they would be available on British production cars. The type developed for the Saladin was basically a steel ring-plate placed against the inner edge of the drum's braking surface, with the breaking effort supplied by floating callipers. Not only did they meet the demand for greater stopping power, but because the Saladin was required to have a deep fording capability, a type of brake was needed that worked more efficiently after immersion than a drum brake. But despite the introduction of conventional drum brakes on the Saracen, which would also have a fording capability of 7ft, the special brakes were to be an exclusive part of the Saladin's specification.

FV602 AND 603

But there was a long way to go before designs were finalized. Along with the FV601 armoured car, there had been two other vehicles planned in the series, using common running gear. These were the FV602 Armoured Command Post and the FV603 Armoured Personnel Carrier. The Armoured Personnel Carrier had been tried in the Great War, but not followed through. Unless marched, troops were moved to and from battle stations by lorry or train, and smaller detachments would also move or be moved in the same way. In wartime this left them without protection from ambush either from the ground or the air. The Germans used a number of specifically designed personnel carriers, many of them of half-track configuration, and the American M3 International half-track was supplied in great numbers to Allied forces, but these were open-top vehicles also vulnerable to attack. A fully enclosed vehicle as envisaged in the Saracen would give protection.

All three variants were to be fitted with common engines, transmissions and suspension components. The engine would be a Rolls-Royce B80 straight-eight-cylinder, water-cooled petrol engine driving through a five-speed pre-selector gearbox coupled to a single-range transfer box with forward and reverse gears, and a single differential. This arrangement of having the reverse gear facility in the transfer box rather than the gearbox itself was chosen as it was specified that the Saladin should have a driving position at both ends. Thus the vehicle would need a range of gears whichever direction it travelled. Although the FV602 or FV603 would only have one driving position, the reverse gear arrangement would not present any difficulty to the driver and a common item would be cheaper to produce and require the Army to carry fewer spare parts.

The 602 Armoured Command Post was another modern concept. The idea of having a command post that could be moved evolved with the change in the way that war was being fought. The German Blitzkrieg, developed in 1918 as a means of breaking the deadlock in the trenches on the Western Front, had shown how devastatingly effective fast moving troops could be. Obviously the field commanders could not be left behind and so their com-

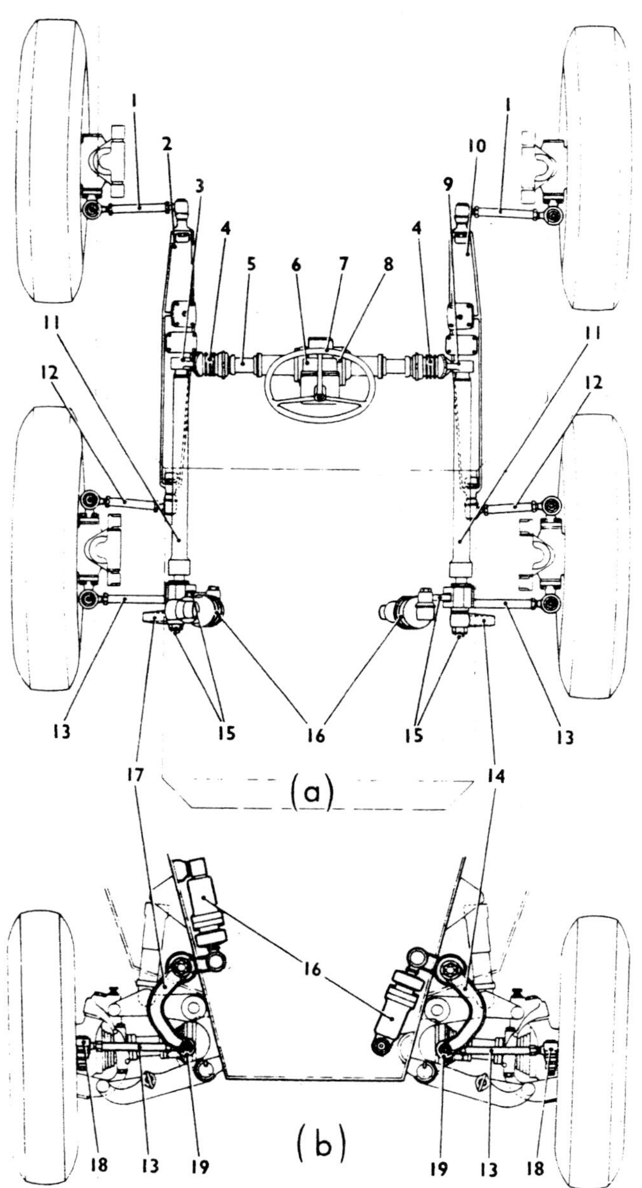

Steering Layout – Front and Centre Axles. (REME Museum)

(a) Plan view
(b) Front view
1 Drag link, centre wheel
2 Steering lever, right hand
3 Cross-shaft, right hand (hand operated)
4 Gaiter covering ball joint
5 Cross-shaft
6 Steering box
7 Steering wheel
8 Steering gear housing
9 Cross-shaft lever, left hand (hand operated)
10 Steering lever, left hand
11 Steering shaft
12 Drag link, front wheel (rear)
13 Drag link, front wheel (front)
14 Drop arm, left hand
15 Drop arm shaft with integral lever (power operated)
16 Steering jacks (hydraulic)
17 Drop arm, right hand
18 Ball socket (ball-joint) right-hand thread
19 Ball socket (ball-joint) left-hand thread

How the Steering Works
The top half of the diagram shows the steered wheels in plan view, with the front wheels at the bottom. Just behind the points where the cross-shaft (5) join the steering levers (2 and 10) are pivots. To make a right-hand turn, the steering wheel moves the cross shaft from right to left, pulling the forward end of the right-hand steering lever to the centre of the vehicle, and at the same time pushing the rear end away. The reverse happens to the left-hand steering lever, with the forward end being pushed away and the rear end moved toward the vehicle. The drag links (1 and 12) act to move the wheels to turn to the right, the front drag links operating behind the front wheels' steering swivels, the centre wheels' drag links operating forward of the swivels. However, note that the pivot point of the steering lever is not central. It is two-thirds of the way along to the rear, and this differential action moves the centre wheels through a much smaller angle.

mand HQs had to be mobile as well. No more would the staff officers be set up in tents or in the comfort of chateaux well behind the lines of a set-piece battle or the years-long stand-off of the Great War. Field Marshall Montgomery took the idea to heart when he commissioned the building of a trailer caravan that would serve as a mobile map room and battle control centre. This vehicle is in the keeping of the Imperial War Museum at Duxford, Cambridgeshire. It was used in Operation Overlord, the Allied invasion of Europe in 1944. In this campaign, Allied company commanders would use such vehicles as jeeps and Dodges fitted with radios. These of course had no armour and, as prime targets, were vulnerable to enemy attack, so a purpose-built mobile command post would need to be armoured like the Personnel Carrier. The 602 was to share the same superstructure as the 603, but it was quickly realized that would not fit the bill. The interior space would be too limited to allow the occupants to stand up and the radios of the time took up too much space. It was soon abandoned.

FV601 DESIGN AND DEVELOPMENT

The FV601 would be the first vehicle to be produced. An initial contract for the supply of drawings for its design and development, and that of the general driveline design was awarded to Alvis in October 1947. Towards the end of the D&D phase there was the allocation of a production contract, but so many sets of all the drawings produced had to be made available to possible other sub-contractors. These were produced so that the other companies could tender for production contract, as the awarding of a D&D contract to one company didn't automatically mean they would get the production contract. There was a second reason. The production contracts would be for the British Army's needs in peacetime or in small-scale conflicts, and for any export orders that might be won. But the memory of the war was still very close, as was all the experience gained with the Shadow Factory scheme of the late 1930s, whereby the British motor industry built new factories with the intent of producing arms and armaments should war break out. As the Cold War loomed ever closer those vehicle manufacturers invited to tender might also be required to produce vehicles under wartime contracts.

It was envisaged that the FV601 would carry a crew of four: a commander, a driver, a gunner and a loader. The proposed main armament for the FV601 was a 2 pounder high-velocity gun, known as the pipsqueak. The idea of fitting a light gun similar to that fitted to the smaller four-wheel Daimler armoured car was that it and the rounds it would carry would keep the weight of the vehicle low, below 10 tons. Nor would sufficient rounds take up too much space inside. But the size of the main gun was causing concern. The 2 pounder was both too small for its application, and also it was unable to fire high explosive (HE) ammunition. However, the FVRDE realized that although the FV601 was one of the biggest purpose-built armoured cars yet to be designed in Britain, it was not strong enough to carry any of the existing larger guns. The 3in (76mm) howitzer fitted to the Churchill tank was of a realistic size but it was way too inaccurate. The Armament Design Establishment at Fort Halstead had a new 76mm gun under development, but it would be five years before it would be ready. A .50in coaxially mounted machine gun would be fitted to the turret and it was also decided at this time that the vehicle commander would have a .50 machine gun mounted on his cupola for anti-aircraft defence.

In January 1949 Alvis's sales director, S.W. Horsfield, was able to tell his board that they were 'likely to be invited to become the "parent firm" in whatever production plans were formulated for the armoured car which we were now in the course of developing'. Nine months later, on 15 and 16 September, a preview and user meeting took place at Alvis, where representatives of the armed services were favourably impressed with the mock-up FV601, which had been under construction since April 1948. Under Captain Smith-Clarke, Alvis began design work on the prototype of the new vehicle. The drawing office, under Willie Dunn's direction, translated the specifications into working plans from which a wooden mock-up was made. From there the experimental department produced the first prototype, the FV601A.

Although the design followed the MoS specifications closely, there were some areas where latitude was allowed. The suspension was to be either coil springs or torsion bars and Alvis opted for the latter. Rubber had been tried as a suspension medium in pre-war cars and was considered for the FV600 series. However, the weight of the proposed vehicles, at around 10 tons, was considered too heavy for a material still largely unproven for the task and would not allow the extensive wheel travel required on a cross-country vehicle.

Captain Smith-Clarke retired from Alvis in November 1949, although the company retained him in a consultancy basis. His place as chief engineer in charge of fighting vehicles would be taken by Willie Dunn. The chairman and managing director, John Parkes, was hopeful that a contract would be awarded very soon for the armoured car. The procurement process, having gone from development and design to approval by the Treasury, had come to a standstill. Despite pressure from the Army and from Alvis, who sent a newly prepared brochure, the Treasury would not sanction the contract. The government had promised to supply special machinery and equipment to the value of £280,000, but Alvis would not at this time see this contract. This delay was initially disappointing, but unbeknown to Alvis the government's decision was forced by events in the Far East. Far from compounding the disappointment, these events would be to Alvis's benefit.

3 The Saracen

During the Second World War the Japanese invaded Malaya, then a part of the British Empire. Working behind enemy lines, British Special Forces enlisted the help of the communist Malayan Peoples' Anti-Japanese Army, the MPAJA, which was recruited under their leader Chin Peng from the indigenous Chinese population. When the Japanese surrendered, the communists attempted to take power in Malaya, but the Malay people, constituting the majority of the population, did not want either communists or the Chinese minority in power.

The British, in line with the policy of gradually bringing independence to the countries of the Empire, would not leave Malaya to fend for itself, but wished to ensure that a stable, democratic system in sympathy with Westminster was firmly in place. Although recognized as a legal entity, the new Malayan Communist Party led an armed revolt. Renaming themselves as the Malay Races Liberation Army (MRLA) they went back into the jungle that covered four-fifths of the country to fight a guerrilla campaign. At first they had the upper hand. The police were under-strength and under pressure and the only British Army presence was a number of Gurkha units, which were undergoing reorganization.

In June 1948 the High Commissioner for Malaya, Sir Henry Gurney declared a state of emergency and in 1950 Sir Henry requested the retired Lt Gen Harold Briggs to plan, co-ordinate and direct the anti-bandit operations of the police and fighting forces. Briggs' plan was 'to dominate the populated areas to build up a feeling of security, which would eventually encourage a flow of information on the Communists in populated areas, and to seek and destroy insurgents by forcing them to attack on ground of security forces' own choosing.' Sir Henry established an integrated police and army organization under a Chief of Intelligence, with joint decisions taken between police and Army.

The terrorists were being supplied by some half a million Chinese living in villages – kampongs in the Malay language – close to the jungle where they were in a position to give assistance to the guerrillas. A food denial policy was instigated to starve out terrorists. The kampongs were cleared out and the inhabitants first moved to special camps with clinics and schools, and then resettled in 500 new villages, surrounded by wire fences, where they were given protection from intimidation by the communists.

In 1951 Sir Henry Gurney, the High Commissioner for Malaya, was murdered in an ambush. He was replaced by Gen Sir Gerald Templer, who integrated police and army activity. He would pursue a 'hearts and minds' policy to involve the whole population in the fight, causing as little disruption as possible to their daily lives and trying to prevent at all costs any civilian casualties. General Sir Gerald would not pour more British troops into the jungle, but rely on a newly raised Home Guard.

Essentially the work in Malaya would be an anti-terrorist campaign in terrain suited to ambush and close-quarter fighting. Heavy artillery and tanks would be useless in the jungle; the need would be for infantry, backed by armoured cars and carried in transport that offered protection

An early production Mk1 Saracen. This vehicle is photographed alongside the A45 Coventry bypass. (Roland Andrews)

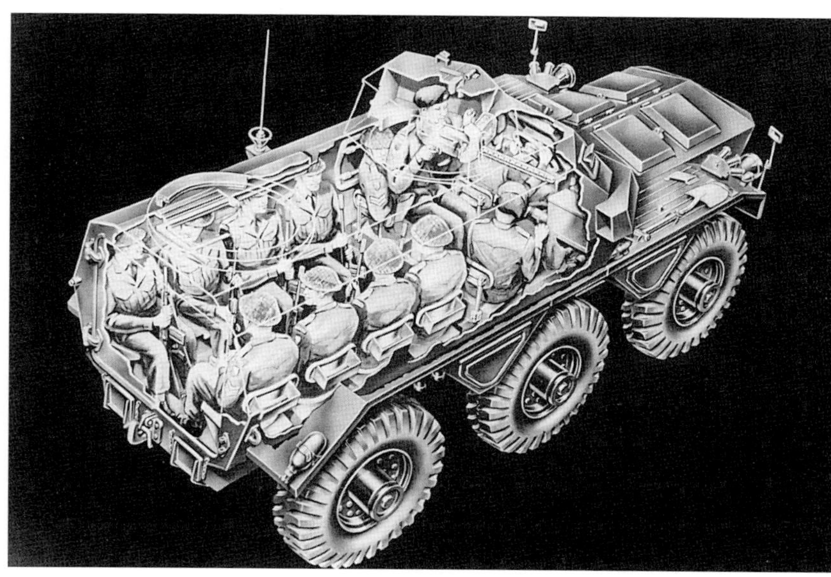

The Saracen in cutaway, showing its troop carrying capacity. The vehicle commander is seen in the turret, manning the machine gun. (Tank Museum, Bovington)

from surprise bandit attack. As the British Army had no fully armoured personnel carriers, the FV603, untried, let alone in production, presented itself as an ideal vehicle in Malaya to work with armoured car regiments escorting food convoys and patrolling rubber plantations. Thus the process of putting the 603 into production was brought forward in place of the Saladin.

On the basis of Alvis's experience and their status as parent firm, they were awarded a production contract for the FV603, named the Saracen in keeping with the FV601's name. Prototypes of the FV603 were produced and presented to the Ministry of Supply in June 1950. By October the Ministry instructed Alvis to proceed with the production of 150 FV603 armoured personnel carriers, with possible need for a total of 600. By November the order had grown to 275, with the maximum likely order being for a further 500. This would be the biggest single order for fighting vehicles that Alvis had ever received. Indeed, this figure was comparable to the production run of some of Alvis's more popular car models of the 1930s!

VEHICLE SPECIFICATION

The mechanical specification was based on that of the Saladin. The engine would be a straight-eight Rolls-Royce B80 petrol engine. This would be coupled via a fluid flywheel to a semi-automatic gearbox with five forward speeds and a forward-and-reverse single-speed transfer box with a 2.43:1 ratio. Also in common with the FV601, it should have six wheels with steering on the front and centre wheels and fully independent suspension on torsion bars. Wheels would 8.00 × 20 WD pattern pressed-steel divided disc, attached by left-hand threads on the nearside, right-hand threads on the offside. Tyres would be 11.00 × 20 run-flat type L.

The obvious difference was the layout, demanding a front-mounted engine, with the driver centrally placed 'astride' it to allow a maximum field of vision. Vision for the driver would be through front and side flaps and he would also have an escape hatch. He would sit in a hull of 'special design', sealed from the ingress of water. Two rear doors would provide access for personnel and emergency hatches would be provided on each side of the vehicle, jettisonable by a quick-release device. Eight small-arms ports would be provided, four on each side, for use by most of the ten personnel that would be transported.

Engine access lids would be provided, fitted with louvred air outlets. The radiator air-intake would be at the front, louvred to prevent damage from shrapnel and stones. The hull should have adequate ventilation when in the 'closed down' situation, with electric induction fans. External stowage containers would be fitted.

The vehicle would have to be capable of towing a laden 1-ton trailer. 'Every effort', the specification demanded, 'shall be made to ensure that the vehicle can be utilized for Phase II airborne, sub-zero, tropical and wading operations with the least degree of preparation.' Lashing eyes and lifting eyes would be fitted to secure the vehicle during transportation.

The total gross weight would be 10 tons (10,170kg), the total basic weight 8 tons 10cwt (8,645kg) The vehicle should not exceed 6ft 6in (1.98m) in height (to the top of the hull), 15ft 11in (4.85m) in length and 8ft 3in (2.51m) in width over wings. The minimum ground clearance should be 1ft 4in (0.41m), the maximum track 6ft 8in (2.03m), wheelbase from front to rear axles 10ft (3.05m) and the front and rear approach angles 50 degrees.

The maximum road speed forward should be 42.8mph (69km/h) at the engine's top governed speed of 3,750rpm, and the average speed should be 27.5mph (44km/h) on hard roads and 20mph (32km/h) cross-country. It should be capable of surmounting a vertical obstacle of 1ft 6in (0.46m), climb a maximum gradient of 24 degrees, have a turning circle of 45ft (13.7m), a side overturn angle of 45 degrees and the ability to cross a 5ft (1.5m) wide trench without the use of channels. It should be able to cross a 3ft 6in (1.1m) ford unprepared and a 6ft 6in (2m) ford with preparation. Its 50gal (190ltr) fuel tank should give a range of 250 miles (400km) at 5mpg (2.12km/ltr) on hard roads, and a fuel consumption of 3mpg (1.28km/ltr) cross-country was expected.

DESIGNING THE SARACEN

Two interesting factors decided the overall dimensions of Saracen. Malaya was one of the world's main producers of rubber, and the rubber trees from which the raw sap is extracted are laid out in precise rows, 8ft (2.45m) apart. These plantations were prime targets for the terrorists and needed to be patrolled. Saracen's overall width was designed so as to fit between the trees of the rubber plantation. An armoured ambulance version was also planned and the length of Saracen would be governed by the longest piece of equipment that the vehicle would be known to carry, a standard NATO stretcher. NATO was then a very new organization, so the equipment at its disposal was that of its constituent armies. Design engineer Fred Phillips laid out the rear of the vehicle taking dimensions from a British Army stretcher that was dated 1918!

With the specification laid out by the War Office, the design work demanded of Alvis was to get the vehicle first to a prototype and then a production standard, and to keep the manufacturing costs to an acceptable level. Although the engine was specified by the MoS, supply of some components was left to Alvis. This is illustrated by the choice of universal joints used in the driveshafts. Rzeppa joints were tried initially, but were too big to fit in the confined length between bevel box and hub, and still allow the wheel articulation desired. Tracta joints were tried and found to be the best available, although for a number of reasons they would not be trouble free.

The Saracen was required to have a fording capability so the hull needed to be watertight. With the transmission shafts placed inside the hull and the articulated driveshafts coming through to the outside, the holes in the hull were sealed around the driveshafts with conventional rubber boots. A greater problem was that of keeping water out of the hubs, and this was solved by designing a grooved housing for an O-ring.

ON TEST

Initial trials of the FV603 prototype, on roads and across country, took place in late spring and early summer of 1951. Its general performance and reliability, its gunnery capability and the effectiveness of its armour all came under scrutiny and the vehicle performed well. It was then delivered to the Army at Cobham on 17 June 1951. The Army and the Ministry of Supply were impressed and wanted delivery as soon as possible. It was recognized that a reasonable time frame had to be in place to procure the components for the vehicle. But British industry was, even after five years, still suffering the effects of the war and suppliers would be unable to deliver materials and components as quickly as either Alvis or the Ministry would have liked.

The urgency with which the Saracen was required demanded that the full test procedures, usually held at Chertsey and other UK locations, be abandoned. Instead, Saracen would be tested in the field, in Malaya. Two vehicles were shipped out by sea in early 1952 and in March Alvis sent one of their engineers, Ron Walton, to supervise the tests and report any shortcomings. There were several.

The first to come to light was the hydraulic system. This powered the brakes and steering and was fully pressurized by a pump driven off the engine. The system incorporated three hydraulic accumulators to boost pressure for manoeuvring the vehicle when engine speeds were low and pressure from the engine-driven hydraulic pump was inadequate. Each accumulator consisted of a rubber bag inside a steel cylinder. The bag was inflated with air to 500psi, which provided the reserve pressure. Provided the fluid surrounding it was pressurized to above 500psi it compressed the bag,

Saracen – Full Technical Description

The Saracen has an all-welded armour-plate steel hull containing the powertrain. Floor plates are 12mm thick, main side lowers are 14mm thick and the sponsons 12mm. Two rear side-opening doors provide access for both crew and personnel. The driver sits in the central front seat with the vehicle commander behind and to the left, the radio operator behind to the left. There is seating for eight troops in the rear, four each side, facing inwards. Most, but not all models were fitted with armaments. These included a turret, with fittings for a Browning .30 machine gun mounted on the roof, with access just behind the driver's seat. A single .303 Bren gun for anti-aircraft duty can be mounted on ring-type mount, with access through a sliding roof-panel toward the rear of the vehicle.

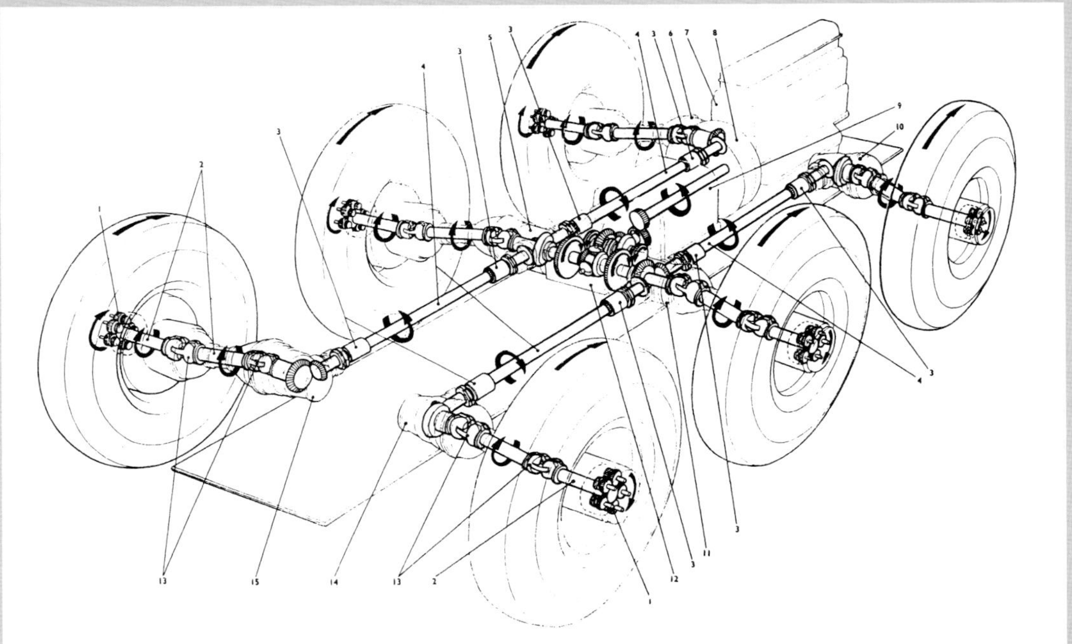

Drivetrain layout

1 Hub reduction gear
2 Articulated axle shaft
3 Transmission shaft coupling
4 Transmission shaft
5 Centre bevel box, left hand
6 Centre bevel box, right hand
7 Engine
8 Fluid flywheel
9 Gearbox
10 Front bevel box, right hand
11 Centre bevel box, right hand
12 Transfer box
13 Tracta universal joints
14 Rear bevel box, left hand
15 Rear bevel box, right hand

The engine is a forward-mounted in-line eight-cylinder Rolls-Royce B80 engine, in the first 250 a Mk3A (aluminium cylinder-head and BSF threads) and in successive models a Mk6A (cast-iron head and UNF threads), coupled to a five-speed Wilson pre-selector gearbox, driving through a centrally placed differential and a forward-and-reverse transfer box. Drive comes outwards from the transfer box to a bevel box adjacent to the centre wheel stations and is taken from the bevel boxes forward and rearward to similar bevel boxes adjacent to the front and rear wheel stations. Drive is then taken via Tracta joints and short driveshafts to the hubs, which contain reduction gears.

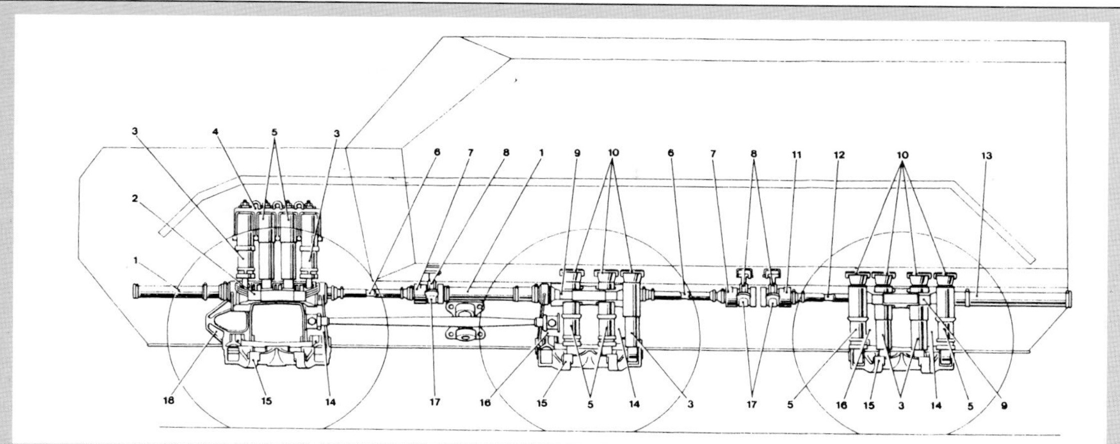

Suspension Layout at Left-Hand Side of Vehicle. Note how the centre and rear shock absorbers and rebound dampers act on the lower wishbones. This is necessary because of the shape of the rear part of the hull.

1 Torsion bar sleeve
2 Top link, front
3 Shock absorber
4 Shock absorber anchor bracket
5 Bump and rebound dampers
6 Torsion bars, left-hand front, left-hand centre and right-hand rear
7 Adjusting lever bracket, right hand
8 Adjuster nuts
9 Top link, centre and rear
10 Damper housings
11 Adjusting lever bracket, right hand
12 Torsion bar, right-hand front, right-hand centre and left-hand rear
13 Torsion bar sleeve, rear
14 Link bracket, right hand
15 Bottom link
16 Link bracket, left hand
17 Adjusting levers
18 Front link bracket, left hand

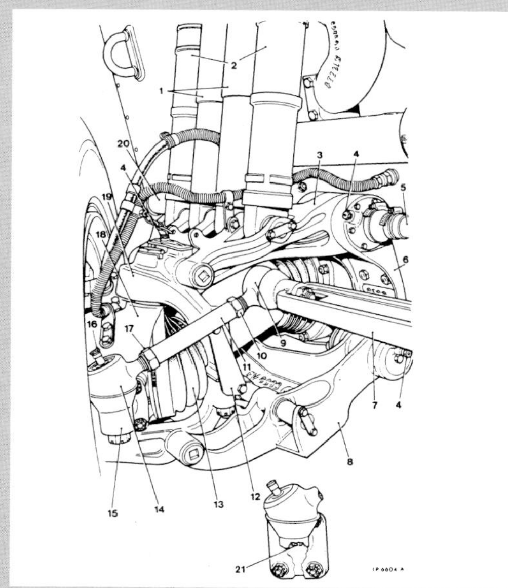

Front Suspension Assembly, Left-Hand Side

1 Bump and rebound dampers
2 Shock absorbers
3 Top link
4 Lubricating nipples
5 Torsion bar
6 Link bracket
7 Steering lever
8 Bottom link
9 Socket assembly (ball joint) left hand
10 Simmond's nut, left hand
11 Drag link tube
12 Cover plate
13 Gaiter
14 Socket assembly (ball joint) right hand
15 Ball joint bracket, front and centre
16 Lubricating nipple
17 Simmond's nut, right hand
18 Hub swivel
19 Swivel yoke
20 Torsion bar sleeve, short
21 Oil level plug (not used)

Saracen – Full Technical Description (*cont.*)

Suspension is independent by double unequal length wishbones on each wheel. The suspension has a total of 10in (253mm) travel, 6½in (165mm) upward travel and 3½in (88mm) rebound. There are two shock absorbers and two rebound dampers per front and rear wheel station and two shock absorbers and one rebound damper per centre wheel station. The forward rebound damper is not fitted, as it would foul the steering rocker.

The steering is a power-operated recirculating ball box, steering the centre and front wheels via a compensating linkage that turns the centre wheels a reduced angle in comparison to the fronts. Brakes are Lockheed drums, power assisted.

raising the pressure within it. When engine speeds were low and the fluid pressure dropped, the increased pressure of the air in the bag maintained pressure in the hydraulic system for a short time. A long sea voyage and driving at low engine speeds had allowed the pressure to drop in the system. Subsequent driving at low hydraulic pressure caused chatter in the control valve, damaging its seating and thus destroying its ability to keep a good pressure seal. Also, after a time at high altitude and in high temperature and humidity, the fluid dissolved the rubber of the accumulator bag, turning it to a black mush.

Another problem occurred in driving the Saracen.

A Mk1 Saracen on test, showing it can handle cross-country work at speed. (Tank Museum, Bovington)

A Mk1 Saracen on convoy escort duty in Malaya. (Tank Museum, Bovington)

The differential was not of a locked type. There were hard tracks and roads in Malaya, but off road there was often soft mud. If a Saracen slipped off the road and the wheels of one side were on loose going, they would lose traction and the locked differential would simply cause them to spin, providing no drive to the wheels on the side where there was good traction. The vehicle would be stranded and have to be winched out.

Further problems arose with the fluid flywheel, gearbox, Tracta joints and transfer boxes, with much of the trouble stemming from the high ambient temperatures. All its life the Saracen would be notorious for being difficult to operate in hot climates, particularly as the floor under the transfer box and the driver's feet would become extremely hot, due in part to the route of the exhaust. Besides, the commander's floor, sited above the overheated transfer box, would get too hot to stand on.

In the early weeks he was in Malaya, a lack of spares made Ron Walton's task more difficult, requiring him and his REME assistants to cannibalize one vehicle to keep the other going. The layout of the vehicle required Walton (and all subsequent REME fitters) to work on the engine from above only, trying to get hands down the small hatches, leaning over armoured bodywork that was made unbearably hot by the tropical climate.

On 30 May 1952 Alvis's production director, H. J. Nixon, presented the first production Saracen to the War Office. That September, with production running at about twenty vehicles per month, the Ministry of Supply told Alvis that 603 production may have to be modified as the situation in Malaya had been stabilized.

Walton returned to England in October 1952 and reported his findings to Alvis, the FVRDE and Rolls-Royce. Praise for Walton and the Saracen

(Above) *Ron 'Soapy' Sutton coaxes the first Saracen through the narrow entrance of the War Office. Note how the wheels had to be raised on wood blocks. This was done so that the hubs could clear the bollards that had been built to prevent carriage wheels from damage on the stonework. (Roland Andrews)*

(Right) *Sutton poses the Saracen in the courtyard of the War Office. (Roland Andrews)*

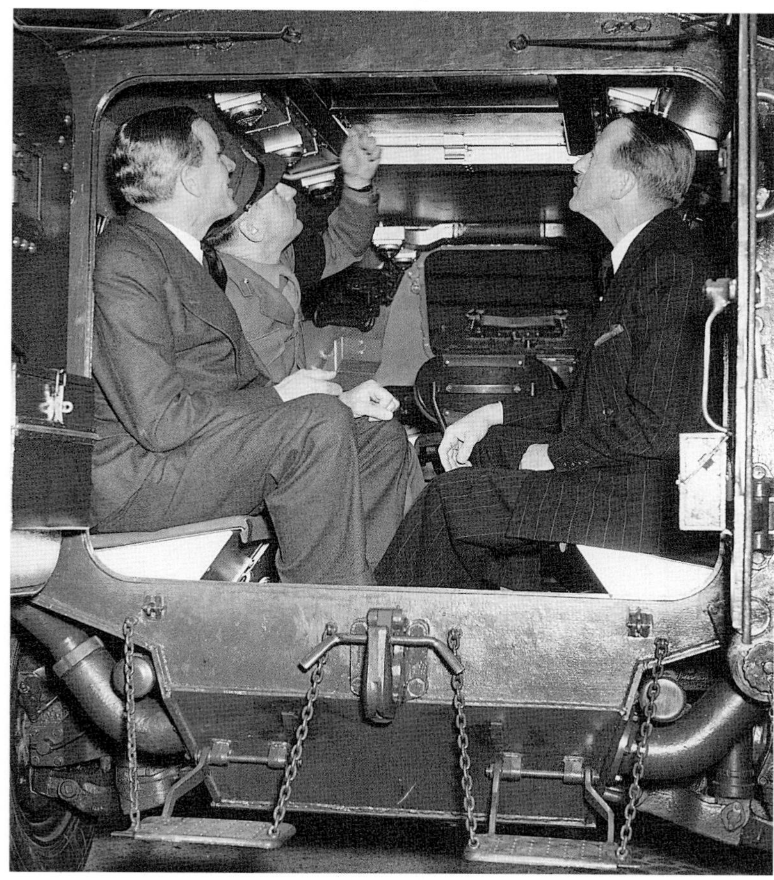

Whitehall top brass examine the Saracen's interior. (Roland Andrews)

came from the very top, Gen Sir Hugh Stockwell, the GOC of FARELF (Far East Land Forces) in Malaya. Writing to Alvis, he described the vehicle's performance as excellent and expressed his appreciation of Walton's work in Malaya.

THE PRODUCTION SPECIFICATION

The FVRDE issued the first specification for the production FV603 in November 1952. Specifying that all versions should use the same basic hull, it called for as many components of the FV601 as possible to be used. The versions of the 603 listed make an interesting comparison with those that eventually would be produced. Covered in detail were four envisaged versions that the FVRDE would want to see first in production.

FV603a Personnel and Load Carrier

For use by the Royal Armoured Corps and Royal Engineers for conveyance of dismounted personnel in Armoured and Armoured Car regiments and in Divisional Engineer units. The interior fittings should be removable from a personnel carrier, to make a load carrier.

Capacity as a personnel carrier would be for either a driver, a section commander and ten passengers or a driver, one NCO, five passengers and 1,000lb of RE stores.

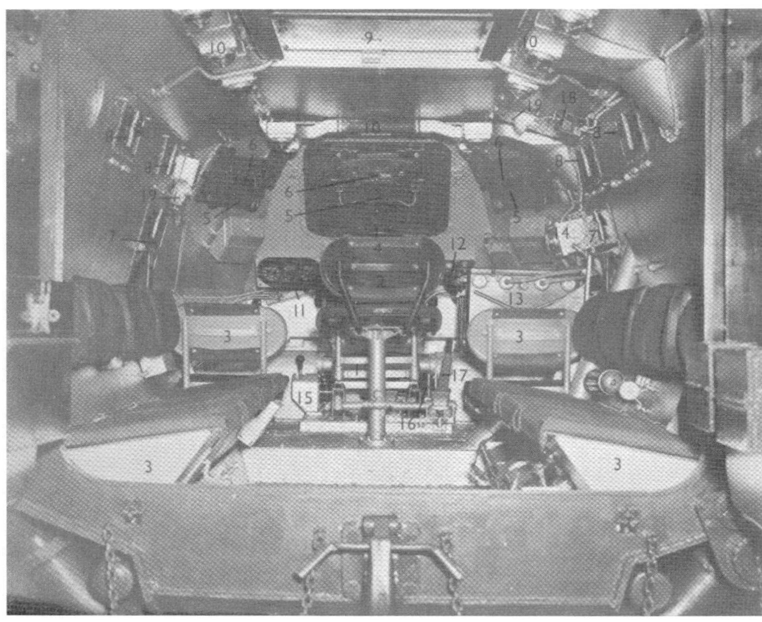

The Saracen's interior detail.
1 Driver's seat
2 Commander's seat, adjustable for height
3 Passengers' seats
4 Driver's escape hatch
5 Driver's visor flaps
6 Driver's periscopes
7 Side escape hatch
8 Small arm ports
9 Sliding roof aperture, with sliding glass and armoured protective panels
10 Interior ventilation ducts
11 Driver's instrument panel
12 Driver's switch panel
13 Two 24v batteries (60 ampere/hours)
14 Master switch
15 Gear selector control
16 Forward and reverse control
17 Mechanical handbrake
18 Firing buttons for smoke dis chargers
19 Three interior lights

Capacity as a load carrier would be a driver and a payload of 2½ tons on roads or 2 tons cross-country.

A 360-degree single-man turret would be provided on the forward end of the hull with a machine gun and an anti-aircraft machine gun should be fitted over a sliding roof window at the rear of the vehicle. Provision should be made for the ammunition required for the platoon carried, being 3,000 rounds of .30 MG ammunition, one 2-inch mortar and twelve rounds of ammunition, and either twelve smoke grenades or one Infantry Platoon anti-tank weapon and twelve rounds of ammunition. A wireless set, No. 19/19B/31 AFV should be provided in each vehicle or a No. 68T set if a No. 31 is not available.

FV603b Regimental Command Vehicle

For use by the Royal Armoured Corps and Signals Regiments. Capacity would be for one driver, two W/T operators and three officers. The vehicle should be divided into a forward compartment occupied by the driver and wireless operators, and fitted with two field wireless sets WS-C40, C11 and B40. The rear compartment, to be known as the Command Compartment, should be fitted with desks and seats for the three officers and additional seating for three more officers. Map boards with a total of 60sq. ft should be provided. The front and rear compartments should be separated by a partition with a sliding hatch, soundproofed to such a level as not to allow the noise of the engine to disturb the occupants of the Command Compartment. Two roof windows with glass and a bulletproof sliding panel would be provided in the hull roof, one for each of the driving and rear compartments, large enough to be used as escape hatches. A wind- and rainproof rear canvas external shelter with closed ends should be carried, which may be erected when the vehicle's rear doors are fully open.

FV603c A.S.S.U. Tentacle Vehicle

For use by Signals Regiments and L/AW for Air Contact Team activities. The vehicle should carry

Saracen – Original FVRDE Specification

Role	
	FV603a Personnel and Load Carrier FV603b Regimental Command Vehicle FV603c A.S.S.U. Tentacle vehicle FV603d Armoured Ambulance (later renumbered as FV606) FV603e Radar Vehicle for use with the Royal Artillery FV603f Sonic Detection Vehicle for use with Signals Regiments and S.W.V. FV603g Infantry Command Post for use with infantry detachments
Engine	
Type	Rolls-Royce B80 Mk 3A in-line eight-cylinder petrol engine, monobloc cast-iron construction. Inlet-over-exhaust valves. Detachable aluminium cylinder head. Dry-sump lubrication
Capacity	5,760cc
Bore	$3^1/_2$in (88.9mm)
Stroke	$4^1/_2$in (114.29mm)
Compression ratio	6.4:1
Power	160bhp at 3,750rpm
Torque	26lb ft at 2,300rpm
Governed speed	3,750rpm
Ignition type	Coil, 24v
Transmission	
Gearbox	Five-speed pre-selector, fluid coupling
Ratios	Top 1.0:1, Fourth 1.61:1, Third 2.64:1, Second 4.73:1, First 8.50:1
Transfer box	Forward and reverse, single range, giving five forward and five reverse speeds
Ratio	2.43:1
Differential	Single, centrally mounted
Propeller shafts	Muff coupling
Bevel box ratio	1.00:1
Axles	Articulating shafts with two Tracta joints per shaft
Hub gearing	4.125:1 double epicyclic
Capacities	
Engine oil	3.5gal (15.9ltr)
Coolant	7.5ga. (34ltr)
Gearbox oil	20 pints (11.36ltr)
Fuel: Main tank	40gal (227.3ltr)
Fuel: Reserve	10gal (45.46ltr)
Brakes	
Foot	Hydraulic, drums on all wheels, hydraulic servo
Hand	Mechanical on all wheels
Servo mechanism	Hydraulic
Steering	
System	Recirculating ball, divided
Servo mechanism	Hydraulic
Suspension	Independent on all six wheels, with unequal length wishbones and longitudinal torsion bars with sleeves giving 10in total travel. Damping by hydraulic shock absorbers and rebound dampers

Saracen – Original FVRDE Specification (*cont.*)

Wheels and Tyres	
Wheels	10.00 × 20 WD pattern divided disc
Tyres	11.00 × 20 Run flat, later increased to 14.00 × 20
Dimensions	
Length (over towing hook)	16ft 4in (5m)
Height to turret	8ft (2.4m)
Height to hull roof	6ft 6in (2m)
Width overall	8ft 3in (2.5m)
Track	6ft 8in (2.1m)
Wheelbase	10ft (3m) overall (5ft, 5ft between axles)
Ground clearance, unladen	1ft 4in (0.4m)
Angle of approach	50 degrees (889 mils)
Turning circle	45ft (13.7m)
Weight (heaviest version)	Unladen 19,040lb (8,640kg) Laden 22,400lb (10,160kg)
Fording Capability	
Shallow unprepared	3ft 6in (1.1m)
Prepared	6ft 6in (2m)
Crew	
APC	Twelve – driver, commander, machine-gun operator and nine passengers
ACP	Eight – driver plus seven command-post personnel
Performance	
Max range at 30mph (48km/h)	240 miles (390km)
Max speed	42.8mph (72km/h) at 3,750rpm
Max safe road speed	27.5mph (44km/h)
Maximum gradient	24 degrees
Vertical obstacle max.	1ft 6in (0.5m)
Trench crossing	5ft (1.5m)
Side overturn angle	45 degrees
Range at average safe road speed	Max 250 miles (400km)
Electrical Equipment	24v negative earth system, with additional charging facilities for special roles and APC vehicles via portable generators mounted on wings
Armament (APC Only)	
Main turret	Browning .30 machine gun No. 2
Roof	.303 Bren gun on ring-type mount for anti-aircraft duty

a driver, three W/T operators, two officers and W/T equipment. Two roof windows with glass and a bulletproof sliding panel would be provided in the hull roof, one for each of the driving and rear compartments, large enough to be used as escape hatches. The hull interior should hold three W/T sets and one auxiliary receiver and suitable seating for the three W/T operators and officers. A total of 30sq. ft of map boards should be fitted, and an external shelter of similar specification to the FV603b shall be provided.

FV603d Armoured Ambulance (later renumbered in this early specification as FV606)

For use by the Royal Armoured Corps and Medical Corps. The vehicle should carry a driver, a medical

The right-hand side of the Mk1, showing two rear doors of the turret. The three rifle ports are in the open position. The mushroom-shaped covers for the ventilation system can be seen; these contain the electric fans. The forward ventilator serves the driver and crew, the rear ventilator the personnel. (Bill Munro)

orderly and either three stretcher cases or eight sitting cases. Two roof windows with glass and a bulletproof sliding panel would be provided in the hull roof, one for each of the driving and rear compartments, large enough to be used as escape hatches. The vehicle shall have standard Red Cross markings. A bulkhead or curtain shall be provided behind the driving compartment. If a bulkhead is fitted, a means of communication between driver and orderly should be provided. Stretchers must be capable of being folded away when sitting cases are carried. The top stretcher should be provided with a quick-loading device.

Three additional versions were identified the specifications of which were to be added at a later date. These were:

- FV603e Radar Vehicle, for use with the Royal Artillery
- FV603f Sonic Detection Vehicle for use with Signals Regiments and S.W.V.
- FV603g Infantry Command Post for use with infantry detachments.

ARMOUR PROTECTION

The armour protection was equivalent to the FV601, being:

- Attack by .5-inch SAAP at a range of 300yd over a frontal arc of 45 degrees
- Attack from 7.92mm SAAP from any direction
- The equivalent of 25-pdr shell splinters at a ground burst 30ft from the vehicle and air burst 50ft from the vehicle
- The detonation, under any wheel, of a mine containing 20lb of explosive
- Protection for the occupants from chemical and biological warfare was also required.

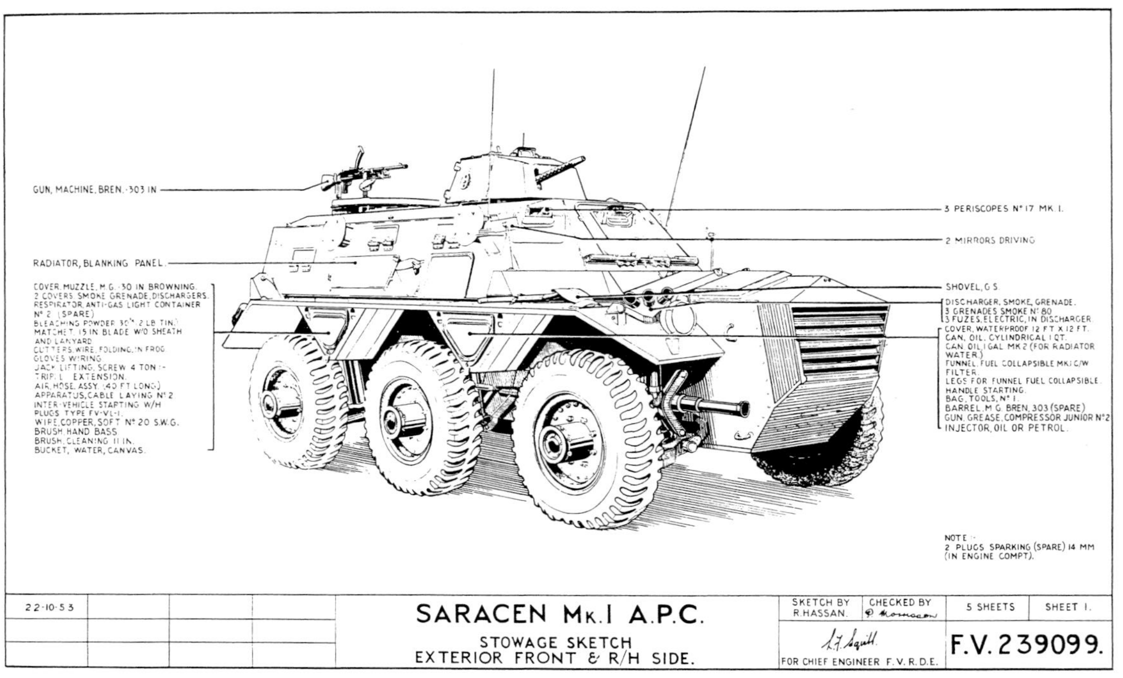

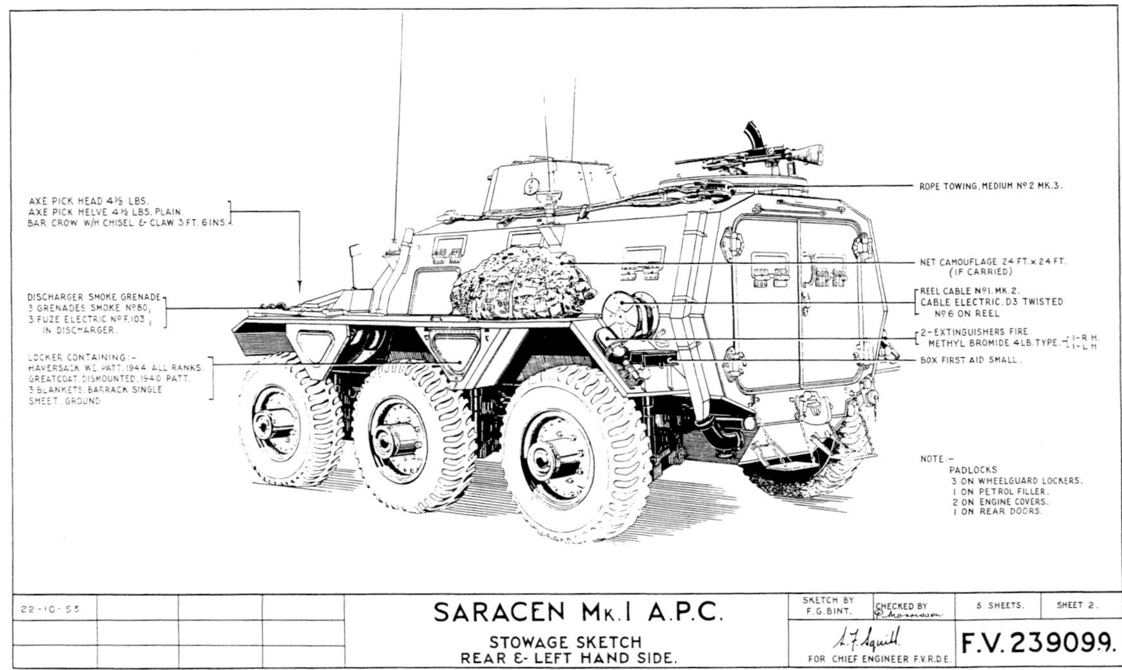

Two views showing the locations of stowed equipment in (above) LHS external and (below) RHS external.

Saracen Mk1 – Technical Specification of Production Model

Role	APC (Armoured Personnel Carrier) for security duties, battlefield reconnaissance and special roles ACV (Armoured Command Vehicle) for use as radio station and special roles
Engine	
Type (first 250 vehicles)	One Rolls-Royce B80 Mk3A in-line eight-cylinder petrol engine, monobloc cast-iron construction. Inlet-over-exhaust valves. Detachable aluminium cylinder head
Type (second 353 vehicles)	One Rolls-Royce B80 Mk6A in-line eight-cylinder petrol engine, monobloc cast-iron construction. Inlet-over-exhaust valves. Detachable iron cylinder head
Lubrication	Dry sump with finned tube oil cooler
Capacity	5,760cc
Bore	3½in (88.9mm)
Stroke	4½in (114.29mm)
Firing order	1-6-2-5-8-3-7-4
Compression ratio	6.4:1
Power	160bhp at 3,750rpm
Torque	257lb ft at 1,700rpm
Governed speed	3,750rpm
Ignition type	Coil, 24v
Transmission	
Gearbox	Five-speed pre-selector, fluid coupling
Transfer box	Forward and reverse, single range, giving five forward and five reverse speeds
Differential	Single, centrally mounted
Propeller shafts	Muff coupling
Axles	Articulating shafts with two Tracta joints per shaft
Hub gearing	4.125:1 double epicyclic
Capacities	
Engine oil	3.5gal (15.9ltr)
Coolant	7.5gal (34ltr)
Gearbox oil	20 pints (11.36tr)
Fuel tank	48gal (218ltr)
Brakes	
Foot	Hydraulic, drums on all wheels, hydraulic servo
Hand	Mechanical on all wheels
Servo mechanism	Hydraulic
Steering	
System	Recirculating ball, divided
Servo mechanism	Hydraulic
Suspension	Independent on all six wheels, with unequal length wishbones and longitudinal torsion bars with sleeves giving 10in total travel. Damping by hydraulic shock absorbers and rebound dampers, two of each per front and rear wheel station, two shock absorbers and one rebound damper per centre wheel station
Wheels and Tyres	
Wheels	10.00× 20 WD pattern divided disc
Tyres	11.00 × 20 Run flat, later increased to 14.00 × 20

Saracen Mk1 – Technical Specification of Production Model (*cont.*)	
Dimensions	
Length (over towing hook)	16ft 4in (5m)
Height to turret	8ft (2.4m)
Height to hull roof	6ft 6in (2m)
Width overall	8ft 3in (2.5m)
Track	6ft 8in (2.1m)
Wheelbase	10ft 0in (3m) overall (5ft, 5ft between wheel centres)
Ground clearance, unladen	1ft 5in (0.4m)
Angle of approach	50 degrees (889 mils)
Turning circle	45ft (13.7m)
Weight, APC unladen	19,040lb (8,640kg)
APC Laden	22,400lb (10,160kg)
Unladen ACP	21,168lb (9,600kg)
Laden ACP	24,640lb (11,180kg)
Bridge Classification	11
Fording Capability	
Unprepared	2ft 7in (0.79m)
With fording plate	3ft 6in (1.1m)
Prepared	6ft 6in (2m)
Crew	
APC	Twelve – driver, commander, machine-gun operator and nine passengers
Performance	
Max range at 30mph (48km/h)	240 miles (390km)
Max speed	45mph (72km/h)
Vertical obstacle max	1ft 6in (0.5m)
Trench crossing	5ft (1.5m)
Electrical Equipment	24v negative earth system, with additional charging facilities for special roles and APC vehicles via portable generators mounted on wings
Armament (APC Only)	
Main turret	Browning .30 machine-gun No. 2
Roof	.303 Bren gun on ring type mount for anti-aircraft duty
Associated Equipment	
Radio installation	19/19B/31 or 19/19B/68T as an interim installation

MALAYAN CRISIS: ESCALATION AND STABILIZATION

General Sir Gerald Templer's plan had begun to stabilize the emergency situation in Malaya, but of course the need for British troops, and thus the equipment they would require, was reduced. This did not affect a plan to involve Crossley Motors, who were invited to tender for a production contract to run parallel with Alvis. But R.W. Rutledge, Alvis's financial director, stressed the need for the Ministry of Supply to 'recognize Alvis as the parent concern in the event of the Ministry deciding to place orders for the 601/603'.

In February 1953 examples of the first production Saracens were sent to Malaya where, despite some expected teething troubles, they met with approval of the troops. It would not be long before the serving regiment would be equipped with them. The Saracen would come off Alvis's production line initially in two basic variants: an APC, distinguished by its turret, and the ACP, which was turret-less. The concept of armoured load carriers was abandoned, but the various command post requirements as defined in the original specification would be met by modifications carried out by the different regiments that were allocated the vehicles.

IDENTIFYING DIFFERENT SARACEN MODELS

It would be prudent at this point to explain the two methods used to identify the different marks of the Saracen and how they will be used in this book. As far as the first version was concerned, Alvis and the FVRDE would call it the FV603A and the Army would call it the Personnel Carrier Mk1. Successive versions would be identified by Alvis and the FVRDE by suffix letters that were relevant only to the mechanical specification and/or the basic hull design. But as various modifications were made to the vehicles by the Army, different Army mark numbers, Mk1, Mk5 and so on, would be used that would not necessarily have a direct equivalent to the Alvis/FVRDE numbers. Where Army versions are discussed, the Army numbering system will be used and where generic models are dealt with, Alvis/FVRDE numbers will be used. It must also be understood that Rolls-Royce had mark numbers, for example Mk3A, Mk8A, for the B-series engine and these should not be confused with the mark numbers of the vehicles in which they were installed.

A problem encountered in production was the move by Rolls-Royce from BSF to UNF thread patterns in their engines. The principal reason for the change was that the British motor industry was being forced by government to export as much of its output as it could and the biggest market was America, which virtually demanded UNF threads. The first engine specified for the Saladin, the No.1 Mk3D and all versions of the B-series up to Mk4, had BSF threads. The first 250 Saracens, being MkI/FV603A, were ordered with Mk3A engines, which had aluminium cylinder heads. It is not known whether all were thus fitted, but subsequent vehicles would have Mk6A engines with iron heads and this engine was made with UNF threads. REME engineers, charged with maintaining all British Army vehicles, could look through their manuals and know that, after a certain number, a particular FV600 type would be UNF.

4 Saracen Development

The Mk2 Saracen's drop-down rear turret door has practical uses! The vehicles are normally driven with the hatches open and only closed down in combat. (Tank Museum, Bovington)

In June 1953 Ron Walton returned to Malaya for further troubleshooting and the following November he was joined by representatives of the FVRDE. The vehicles were by this time in service with the 11th Hussars, the 15/19th Hussars, 221st Vehicle Battalion, RASC and the 17th Gurkha Infantry division. Examples of a new FV603B/Mk2 Saracen were to be sent out to Malaya: 82 BA 16 and 00 BB 12 went to the 15/19th Hussars and 00 BB 21 went to the 11th Hussars. Two more Mk2s, 82 BA 66 and 00 BB 15 were also sent, but not issued at this time to regiments. The FV603B, Personnel Carrier Mk2 differed from the 603A/Mk1 in just two ways. Whereas the Mk1 turret had two side-opening rear doors, the Mk2 had one drop-down rear door, done simply because it worked as well as, if not better than the original design and was slightly cheaper to make. The other involved the unreliable air-bag-type hydraulic accumulators that, after some considerable negotiation with Lockheed, were replaced by a piston type on the Mk2. The Saracen performed well in Malaya, although suffering from fuel starvation problems when climbing steep hills on the mountainous tracks, which was attributed to the long, flat fuel tank.

Since the company began building fighting vehicles, overseas sales had been very important to them. Things looked hopeful on the export front when a Saracen was demonstrated to the US Government Department for Offshore Contracts. They were contemplating the opportunity to buy examples for NATO, whilst representatives of the other members of NATO, including staff from Canada, Belgium, West Germany, Greece, Holland and Norway would have a demonstration of their own in May of 1953. South Africa was another country showing interest and some of the 500-odd examples anticipated for delivery to the Ministry of Supply would be sent there.

OTAC, the Ordnance Tank-Automotive Command, based in the Detroit Arsenal in Michigan, in America's automobile heartland, was the US Army's body for designing and procuring new vehicles. In July 1954 they took delivery of an FV603B, vehicle number 506, 81 BA 79, to, in their own words, 'evaluate any unusual design features which might warrant consideration in future US wheeled vehicle design'. The following year this FV603 was transferred to the Army Engineers at Fort Knox where it was compared to its much heavier contemporary, FMC's M59 tracked personnel carrier. The US Army's engineers liked the Saracen's soft ride, its ventilation system and the way the driveline layout allowed for a low profile, but found that it was not an easy vehicle to work on. It was returned to Detroit, where OTAC continued to study it, arriving at the conclusion that its driving position was uncomfortable and its driveline noise was unacceptable. No sales of the FV603 were made to the USA, but the Americans achieved what they were after; an assessment of the vehicle for their own information.

REVERSE FLOW COOLING

The most visually noticeable modification to the Saracen dealt with the operation of the vehicle in high temperatures. The Middle East Land Forces (MELF) reported to the FVRDE that the inside of the Saracen was unbearably hot in desert climates. In July 1955 two Mk2 Saracens, 00 BB 30 and 00 BB 31, originally earmarked for the delayed Operation *Return Ticket*, were modified and sent to Libya for independent trials. These would be conducted by J Battalion, RHA, firstly at Homs, and later some 70 miles (110km) inland in the desert sands at Beni Ulid.

Heat from the engine and the radiator coming into the vehicle interior was the main cause of the overheating. Modifications were made to reverse the flow of cooling air through the radiator, pushing it out of the front of the vehicle instead of through ducts around the sides. This was achieved by fitting Saladin fans, which operated in the reverse direction to the Saracen's, and by fitting a blank plate across the air intake. The top of the front panel was modified to direct the air blown forward out of the radiator over the bonnet. The rear engine covers on the bonnet were adapted to be partially raised so as to allow cooling air to enter the engine compartment, and the turret was to be reversed and the top hatch kept open to act as an air intake for the crew compartment.

The vehicles were tested over a thirteen-day period, covering an average of 1,400 miles (2,240km) each over desert tracks, main roads and soft sand, with crews of between four and five men. With no convoy to slow their progress each vehicle achieved quite high average speeds. The test results were hampered by lower than expected ambient temperatures, caused by offshore winds, and it was only on the last days that the temperature reached the hoped for 120°F (49°C).

Naturally some shortcomings were found in the modifications to the cooling system, as would be expected in an experimental set-up. The air coming out of the front of the cowling was being blown back into the fresh air intakes of the passenger compartment and, when they were open, through the firing ports. It was also re-entering the engine compartment when the air intake covers were open. However, the air temperature was noticeably lower, both in the crew compartment and, thanks to the air flowing under the vehicle at speed, below the driver's left foot, where the exhaust had been heating the floor to an intolerable level.

As an additional part of these tests, one set of larger 14 × 20 tyres was tried, fitted on one vehicle at first and then the other, to assess their performance and to obviate any discrepancies between

One of the Mk2s used in the hot weather trials in Libya. (Tank Museum, Bovington)

the two vehicles. They proved successful in preventing the heavy vehicle from sinking into soft going. The increased rolling radius of these tyres also improved the top speed and the fuel consumption, by effectively reducing the engine speed. This also reduced the engine's operating temperature and thus reduced the interior temperature of the vehicle.

The results of these trials established what needed to be done to enable a Saracen to operate

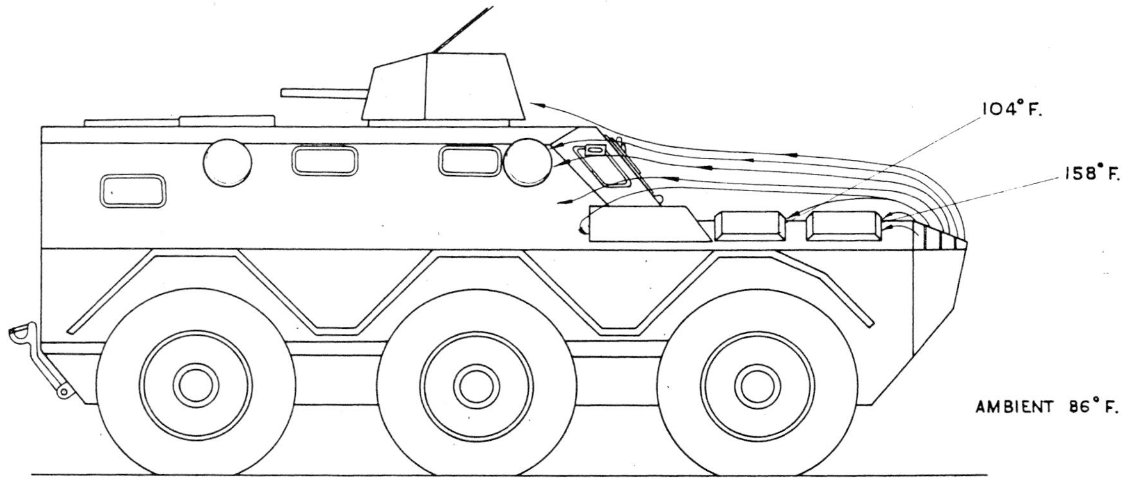

This diagram from the FVRDE shows the airflow created by the modifications made to the Saracens in the hot weather trials.

On the beach at Aden, a Mk2 Saracen fitted with the experimental RFC set-up. The air outlets are visible on the top of the front cowling. This picture was taken at least five years after the Libya trials – note the Series II Land Rover in the background, a vehicle that was not made until 1958. (Tank Museum, Bovington)

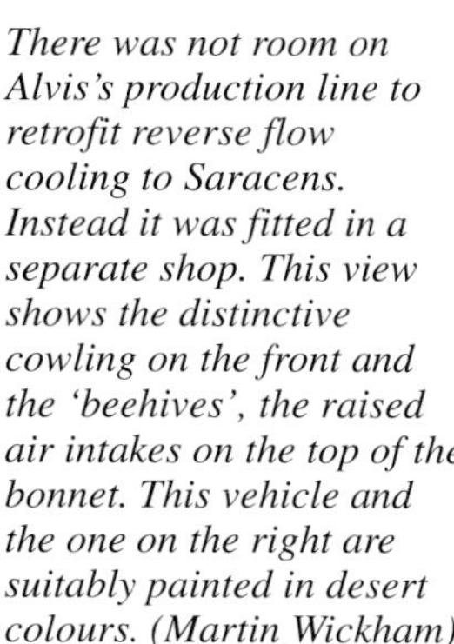

There was not room on Alvis's production line to retrofit reverse flow cooling to Saracens. Instead it was fitted in a separate shop. This view shows the distinctive cowling on the front and the 'beehives', the raised air intakes on the top of the bonnet. This vehicle and the one on the right are suitably painted in desert colours. (Martin Wickham)

in desert climate. Alvis were asked to take the findings of the trials in Libya and produce an effective design of reverse flow cooling (RFC). The rear pair of engine access lids was replaced by what were termed 'beehives' – louvred boxes built into the access lids that acted as air inlets. The air drawn in from the beehives was blown through the radiator. It hit deflectors that ducted it downwards and outwards. Two detail problems faced Alvis's engineers. One was armouring the beehives to prevent bullets or shrapnel entering the engine compartment and damaging the engine. This was achieved, after a considerable amount of work, by placing baffles inside the beehives. Also, when the vehicle was stationary the hot air coming out of the front would blow over anyone standing close by. A large sheet-rubber deflector and sheet-metal deflector plates were placed below the front cowling area to direct it downwards and outwards.

RFC was fitted in the factory to Mk2 vehicles and these were renumbered FV603C by the FVRDE.

COLD WEATHER

But if the Saracen was susceptible to problems in hot weather it was happier in the cold. Winter trials of a Saracen, 05 BB 43, took place at Fort Churchill, Manitoba, Canada between November 1956 and March 1957. Temperatures down to –35°F (–37°C) presented no problems to it.

TOGGLING UP

The Wilson pre-selector box used in three of the FV600 models was a semi-automatic transmission. The driver would change gear by first selecting the gear wanted immediately before he needed it. He then changed the gear by depressing the gear selector pedal, which is where the clutch would be in a vehicle with a manual gearbox. This 'pre-selecting' operation gave the gearbox its name. The box incorporated epicyclic gear sets, each of which consisted of a cluster of small gears set around the gear shaft, running inside an internally toothed ring gear. To make the gear changes, a friction-lined band would either grip or release the outer surface of a ring gear, which altered the ratio of the gear set. The linings of the bands were prone to wear and to accommodate this an automatic adjusting mechanism was incorporated.

The work placed on the gearbox in a Saracen was much more stressful than that of a large Daimler car or RT-type London bus (fully laden the Saracen was almost as heavy as a full bus) where pre-selector boxes were most commonly found. In consequence the bands wore out at a rate faster than that with which the adjusting mechanism could cope. To compensate, the driver had to 'toggle up' before driving off the first time each day. This operation consisted of changing up and down through the gears whilst the vehicle was stationary. If this operation was not carried out, the gear pedal would kick back violently against the driver's left foot.

HOBBS TRANSMISSION

An alternative transmission was tried on a Saracen in early 1955. The Hobbs Mecha-matic gearbox was a fully automatic gearbox that used mechanical rather than hydraulic or electric changing mechanisms and didn't require 'toggling up', which is perhaps why the FVRDE undertook the tests. Hobbs, who became part of the giant BSA group, had tried their transmission in many applications, including a Jaguar XK120 that was rallied by a member of the Hobbs family, Beardmore and Austin taxis, and a Lanchester saloon car, but reliability problems dogged it. The Saracen trials were no more successful, a clutch plate fracturing and seizing the box. Trials were abandoned.

ARMOURED COMMAND VEHICLES

Originally the FV602 Armoured Command Vehicle was planned as part of the FV600 programme, but this version was not followed through as it was felt that the hull wasn't capacious enough for the job. One reason was that the radios in use at the time were bulky. It was soon realized that such a vehicle would be needed and, as radio equipment

Saracen Mk2 and Further Variants – Technical Specification

(Data common for all types unless specifically indicated)

Engine	
Type	Rolls-Royce B80 Mk6A in-line eight cylinder petrol engine, monobloc cast-iron construction. Inlet-over-exhaust valves. Detachable iron cylinder head
Lubrication	Dry sump with finned tube oil cooler
Capacity	5,760cc
Bore	3½in (88.9mm)
Stroke	4½in (114.29mm)
Compression ratio	6.4:1
Power	160bhp at 3,750rpm
Torque	261lb ft at 2,300rpm
Governed speed	3,750rpm
Ignition type	Coil, 24v
Transmission	
Gearbox	Five-speed pre-selector, fluid coupling
Transfer box	Forward and reverse, single range, giving five forward and five reverse speeds
Differential	Single, centrally mounted
Propeller shafts	Muff coupling
Axles	Articulating shafts with two Tracta joints per shaft
Hub gearing	4.125:1 double epicyclic
Capacities	
Engine oil	3.5gal (15.9ltr)
Coolant	7.5gal (34ltr)
Gearbox oil	20 pints (11.36ltr)
Fuel tank	48 gal (218ltr)
Brakes	
Foot	Hydraulic, drums on all wheels
Hand	Mechanical on all wheels
Servo mechanism	Hydraulic, piston type
Steering	
System	Recirculating ball, divided, hydraulically assisted
Servo mechanism	Hydraulic
Suspension	Independent on all six wheels, with unequal length wishbones and longitudinal torsion bars with sleeves giving 10in (25cm) total travel. Damping by hydraulic shock absorbers and rebound dampers, two of each per front and rear wheel station, two shock absorbers and one rebound damper per centre wheel station
Wheels and Tyres	
Wheels	10.00 × 20 WD pattern divided disc
Tyres	11.00 × 20 Run flat, later increased to 14.00 × 20
Dimensions	603 APC and 604 ACV
Length	Standard cooling 16ft 4in (5m) RFC 17ft 2in (5.2m)
Height to turret	603: 8ft (2.4m)

Saracen Mk2 and Further Variants – Technical Specification (*cont.*)

Height to hull roof	603, 604: 6ft 6in (2m) 610: 8ft 4½in (2.52m)
Width overall	8ft 3in (2.5m)
Track	6ft 8in (2.1m)
Wheelbase	10ft (3m) overall (5ft between axles)
Ground clearance, unladen	1ft 5in (0.4m)
Angle of approach	Mk2 50 degrees (889 mils) Mk3 53 degrees (942 mils)
Turning circle	45ft (13.7m)
Weights	
APC Mk2 & 3 unladen	19,040lb (8,636kg)
APC Mk2 & 3 laden	22,400lb (10,160kg)
APC Mk5 & 6 unladen	22,568lb (10,237kg)
APC Mk5 & 6 laden	24,724lb (11,214kg)
ACV Mk2 unladen	19,040lb (8,636kg)
ACV Mk2 laden	22,400lb (10,160kg)
ACP unladen	21,168lb (9,601kg)
ACP laden	24,640lb (11,176kg)
Fording Capability	
Unprepared	2ft 7in (0.787m)
With fording plate	3ft 6in (1.066m)
Prepared	6ft 6in (1.981m)
Performance	
Max range at 30mph (48km/h)	240 miles (386.5km)
Max speed	45mph (72km/h
Vertical obstacle max.	1ft 6in (0.457m)
Trench crossing	5ft 0in (1.524m)
Towing	1 ton trailer facility
Bridging weight	11 ton
Crew	
APC	Twelve – driver, commander, machine-gun operator and nine passengers
ACP	Eight – driver plus seven command post personnel
Ambulance	Two – driver plus one medical orderly
Electrical Equipment	24v negative earth system. Vehicle battery charging is by two-speed 75amp/hour DC generator, later replaced by 90amp/hour AC charging equipment. Additional charging facilities for special role and APC vehicles via portable generators mounted on wings
Armament (APC Only)	
Main turret	Browning .30 machine gun No. 2 (Mk1 vehicle) or No. 4 (Mk2 vehicle)
Roof	.303 or 7.62mm Bren gun on ring-type mount for anti-aircraft duty
Associated Equipment	Radio installation B47, C11, C13, C42, C45, R209, R210 FACE (Field artillery computer equipment) installation Green Archer sound ranging post Radar no 14, Mk1 installation Ambulance installation
Air Portability	
	One vehicle per Hercules Three vehicles per Belfast

An FV603 ACV. (Tank Museum, Bovington)

The FV604 Armoured Command Vehicle uses 'wings' and 'penthouse' extensions to the hull to mount the canvas extension. This model, without a turret, has the anti-aircraft gun ring moved forward. (Tank Museum, Bovington)

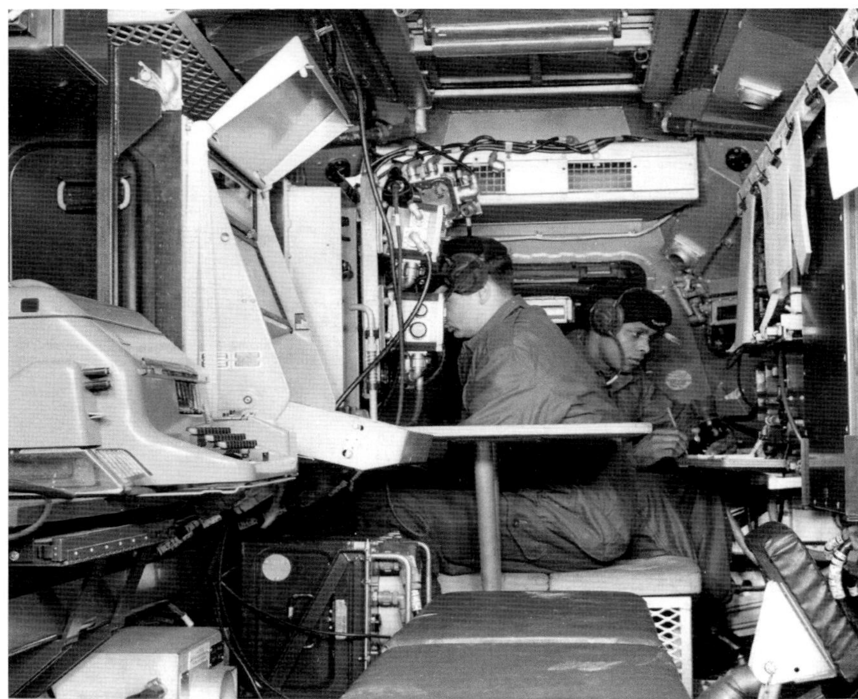

The interior of an FV604. Compare this with the space in an FV610 AcoP (shown later in this chapter). (REME Museum)

had improved, a new Armoured Command Vehicle was built based on, first, the Mk1 and later the Mk2 Saracen. This vehicle would be without a turret as there would be no room for the commander's seat inside from which he would operate the gun. It would carry either the .303in or the 7.62mm NATO standard machine gun. A generator was carried externally and a canvas extension was erected at the rear of the vehicle to give greater space for the command post crew of seven (excluding driver) to operate. The vehicle would not have a separate Army mark number but be referred to as an ACV Mk1 or Mk2 depending on the mechanical specification of the base vehicle.

The Royal Armoured Corps would also convert some FV603Bs to ACVs for use as signals vehicles. Some retained the turret but those that did not had the anti-aircraft gun mounting ring moved forward to where the turret had been. The conversions would be numbered as the FV604 Armoured Command Vehicle.

APPLIQUÉ ARMOUR

Some Mk1 and Mk2 vehicles were fitted with appliqué armour to the front of the wings for use as training vehicles. Vision blocks, which replaced the No. 17 periscopes, were fitted in the driver's hatch to prevent a bullet being fired directly into the driver's face. These vehicles were re-designated as Mk1/5 and Mk2/5 respectively. Full appliqué armour included covering of the firing ports. Full appliqué armour was also fitted to some FV603Cs. The Army numbered these vehicles, which it will be remembered had reverse flow cooling as standard, as the Mk6.

ARMOUR PLATE PROBLEMS

In 1961 Beardmore, the supplier of armour plate to Alvis, announced that they would be closing their Glasgow works. Once the largest industrial con-

This FV604 ACV has appliqué amour, which can be seen over the rifle ports, and also vision blocks for the driver. (REME Museum)

cern in Scotland, they were originally under the control of the Beardmore family. They had been steel manufacturers for over 100 years, had been makers of armour plate for most of that time and, following a disastrous period in the 1920s, had been taken over by Vickers. Stocks of eight sets of armour plate sheets for reserve and twenty-two sets for a contract for Jordan would be bought in until a new supplier was contracted.

SOUTH AFRICA

In May 1956 Ron Walton, now Alvis's service manager, visited the South African Army with two men from the FVRDE, A.A. Sykes and the deputy director of wheeled vehicles, W.J. Semms. The visit was to verify the complaints experienced by the South Africans with the Saracen, the Saladin, the Ferret scout car, the Centurion Tank and its transporter. They were also there to answer questions about a new model under development, the FV651 Fire Crash Tender. The South Africans made the British contingent welcome, pleased that they were taking their problems seriously.

The South Africans were operating Saracens from Port Elizabeth at an altitude of 4,000ft (1,200m) and were suffering from overheating problems due to the lower barometric pressure. Although the engine temperature was higher, there was no problem from fuel vaporization, which had dogged the vehicle when operating in desert climates. Driver discomfort, highlighted by the South African representatives, was to be an ongoing problem with the Saracen. In this case the problem was the now familiar one of the heat created by the exhaust pipe passing under the floor below the driver's left foot.

A Mk1 Saracen of the South African Army. (Tank Museum, Bovington)

SARACEN OVERSEAS SALES

Alvis were allowed to sell directly to overseas customers but as part of the price had to bear a burden of charge to the government because they were responsible for the initial funding of the design and development work on the vehicle. More overseas interest in Saracen was shown, with trials in Canada and Holland. Arrangements to demonstrate the vehicle to the Swiss government were, however, postponed. There was interest from Australia too, and an order for thirty vehicles was anticipated, which would be supplied by the Ministry out of their outstanding order for 283.

In March 1953 the Ministry of Supply told Alvis that it was reducing its delivery requirements for FV603 as the situation in Malaya was improving. This undoubtedly spurred Alvis's sales people to secure export orders. In late 1955 Alvis's chief engineer, Willie Dunn, and the sales manager, S. W. Horsfield, visited the Federal German capital of Bonn to try and sell 2,500 Saracen APCs to the German government. Whilst Horsfield was optimistic, the FV603 was competing in trials the following April with Hotchkiss and Hispano-Suiza APCs. These were tracked vehicles, a type that would be chosen in preference by the Germans, and Alvis were unsuccessful in securing a contract. This was somewhat disturbing to Alvis as the British Government contract was nearing completion and they would be looking for more work.

By 1955 the trouble in Malaya was by no means over, but it had reached a point of stability for which the British government were aiming. The Alliance party under Tunku Abdul Rahman won a free election with a substantial majority. Malaya was now an independent country with a democratically elected government and a part of the British Commonwealth. Military assistance was given to the new Malay government to fight off the remaining Communist terrorists who had refused an amnesty. As far as the FV600 series was concerned, the need for the large numbers first envisaged had been much reduced.

Air portability was not specified by the FVRDE in the 1940s – powered transport aircraft to take anything larger than a light truck were not available. The loss of Empire and the crippling cost of keeping large forces east of Suez brought the need for rapid deployment to the fore. This meant air portability. The introduction to the RAF of the Blackburn Beverley in 1957 and the Armstrong-Whitworth Argosy in 1961 enabled armoured vehicles to be airlifted. A Mk1 Saracen is a tight fit in this mock-up Argosy fuselage. (Tank Museum, Bovington)

Model Identification at a Glance

All Saracens shared the same drive train, suspension and brakes. The first 250 had the B80 Mk3A engine, all others the Mk6D engine. The different versions were as follows:

Models as Identified by the British Army

APC Mk1: Original model APC, turret with one top and two rear doors. Periscopes in the driver's front and side hatches.
APC Mk2: Visually very similar to the Mk1 except that the turret has only two doors, the rear dropping down.
APC Mk1/5, Mk2/5: FV603A/APC Mk1 and FV603B/APC Mk2 respectively, fitted with vision blocks and appliqué armour at left-hand front and right-hand front for training purposes. As the chassis and running gear and the basic hull design was identical to their respective Mk1 and Mk2 versions there was no equivalent Alvis/FVRDE number.
APC Mk3: This is an FV603B/APC Mk2, fitted with reverse flow cooling during production and renumbered FV603C. No Mk1 was fitted with RFC at the factory as the modification was introduced after the Mk1 ceased production.
APC Mk5: FV603B/APC Mk2 with full appliqué armour, new (30G) seat and vision blocks for driver.
APC Mk6: FV603C with reverse flow cooling and full appliqué armour.
ACV Mk1 & Mk2: Armoured Command Vehicle. No turret fitted. Two canvas penthouses carried, which were erected at the rear to accommodate the crew. There is no specific Army mark number or FVRDE number for the ACV.
FV610 ACP: An Armoured Command Post, built for the Royal Artillery. It has a high-sided hull and two canvas penthouses. No turret is fitted. Some have RFC but there is no separate Army mark number for the FV610.
FV611: An Armoured Ambulance, on the basic 603 hull. No turret fitted. There is no specific Army mark number for the FV611.

Alvis/FVRDE Numbers

(*See* Chapter 3 'Identifying Different Saracen Models')

FV603A: Personnel Carrier Mk1, three-door turret
FV603B: Personnel Carrier Mk2, two-door turret
FV603C: Personnel Carrier Mk3, fitted with reverse flow cooling at the factory
FV604: Armoured Command Vehicle (conversion, no specific Army mark number)
FV610: Armoured Command Post
FV611: Armoured Ambulance

As manufacturers and recondition contractors, Alvis had no need to identify the different models beyond the mechanical specification or the structure of, and appendages fitted to, the hull.

Army Conversions

APC: Conversion to radar No 14 (ZB 298).
Ambulance: Conversion of standard APC with facilities for two stretcher and four sitting patients.
Kremlin 1: For internal security duties – converts from Mk2 and 3 to Mk5 and 6 respectively.
Kremlin 2: Additional internal security requirements.
ACV: Converted from basic APC.
ACP FACE: Field Artillery Computer Equipment

The fighting vehicle shop would likely be silent until the end of 1957 when the Saladin was due to come on line, resulting in the layoff of skilled men who might not return. Alvis suggested that production be cut from twenty a month to five, to keep as many men on as possible. But this would be tempered by the likelihood of a new model, the FV610 Armoured Command Post, which would fill the gap. The Ministry of Supply agreed to take a slower delivery of the remaining 603s. Fifty men were laid off, and 200 were put on a four-day week. All fighting vehicle production for the British government was to be completed by the end of 1961 with no prospect of any further orders for the 600 series from the War Office, which from 1959 took over the Army's procurement duties from the Ministry of Supply. Even then production was held up in early 1961 by shortage of free issue items.

Delivery of Saracens to overseas buyers had begun by the end of the 1950s. Alvis and the FVRDE took some time and trouble to ensure that any problems encountered by the vehicles in service, either with the British Army or other governments, were identified and put right in one way or another. Now, with the exception of the new FV651 Salamander Fire Crash Tender for the RAF, these foreign and Commonwealth customers would be the main source of orders for new FV600 vehicles.

South Africa was interested in more FV603s, but the chance to sell was jeopardized by interest from the French Panhard concern, who were trying hard to sell their own fighting vehicles. It caused enough concern for John Parkes to arrange a visit to South Africa to see what could be done. At one point the South African Army were unhappy with the performance of the Saracen. The models sold were Mk1s and the South Africans wanted upgraded vehicles. The issue was further complicated because the government would not make a decision on the vehicles until after the impending election. Most, if not all, of these vehicles were used for internal security work.

The Swiss continued to show interest, asking at the beginning of 1958 for a quote on between 100 and 500 Saracens and Saladins, but in the end decided against both in preference for tracked vehicles. In September 1958 the Sudanese government showed an interest in twenty-five, but there was a delay due to problems within the country's finance department. Eventually forty-nine Saracens were sold to them.

In February 1959 the Dutch asked for a quote for 100 FV604A ambulances, an enquiry which did not result in sales. Although all FV production was slowed by delays in components supply in mid-1959, an order for 176 fighting vehicles was approved. Of these, 134 were destined for Indonesia, but although the actual total is not known exactly, somewhere between fifty-six and seventy-eight were actually delivered.

In June 1963 an order for twenty Saracens for Jordan was confirmed, worth £372,300. These were delivered in 1964, and a further ten were delivered in 1968 with another thirty following in 1969. Another Arab nation who was an important customer for the FV603 was Kuwait, who bought seventy in 1970 and fifty the next year. These were FV603C vehicles with RFC. Some, if not all, were open topped, a version which Alvis had not attempted to build before or after. Sharjah would also buy twelve, Libya seventy, Qatar twenty-five and Bahrain eight. Other African customers were Sudan, who bought forty-nine and Nigeria, who took twenty. Thailand bought twenty and Sri Lanka, then Ceylon, bought twenty-four.

FURTHER SARACEN MODELS

FV610 Armoured Command Post

The Royal Artillery put forward a requirement for a new design of command post vehicle with a high roof. This would become the FV610 Armoured Command Post, known as the ACP and colloquially as ACoP. In April 1957 a contract for the first ten FV610s was received from the Ministry of Supply. They would actually be built from the mechanical components and lower hulls allocated for the remaining ten 603s of an order still in the process of manufacture.

The ACP had a new taller hull, 10½in (265mm) higher than that of the FV603/604. This was made

A prototype FV610. Note the civilian number plate, the unfinished storage compartments and the small generator on the nearside front wing. The higher roof enabled much taller doors to be fitted. The canvas extensions are carried folded on the roof and are hung on the bars on the 'penthouse'-shaped rear panel. (Tank Museum, Bovington)

The production FV610. Note the crew compartment air intakes are relocated to the front. The cage structure on the front wing mounts the auxiliary generator. (Tank Museum, Bovington)

The interior of the FV610. The high roof enabled radios to be carried on racks above the crew's heads, giving room for the fold-down map tables. (Tank Museum, Bovington)

The interior of the FV611 armoured ambulance. Note how the upper stretcher is folded up. Three 'walking wounded' can be carried on the seats seen to the right of the picture. (Tank Museum, Bovington)

from new side panels rather than by extending the existing FV603 components. Like the FV604, provision was made for a canvas extension to the vehicle, giving extra space for operations. RFC was fitted to some FV610 ACPs, although no distinguishing number was given to these variants. The FV610 carried a crew of six, consisting of three staff officers, two radio operators and a driver. Between early 1961 and the end of 1968, 130 were built for the RA, with ten more built for Kuwait in 1970.

Much more equipment could be carried in the FV610 than in the FV604. The additional kit included map boards, communications equipment and an externally mounted auxiliary charging plant. The FV610 could also carry FACE (Field Artillery Computer Equipment). This modification gives some notion of the pace at which technology was coming into the military. The idea of computerized artillery ranging would be almost science fiction to the serving soldier in 1948 when the FVRDE was drawing up plans for the FV600 series.

A Surveillance Radar G.S. No. 9 Mk1, known as 'Robert', was developed and fitted to an experimental FV610. The power for the radar system was carried in a separate trailer.

FV611 Armoured Ambulance

The FV611 was an Armoured Ambulance, six examples of which were built on the basic hull. It could carry either ten seated patients, or three stretcher-borne patients on the left-hand side and two seated patients. The FV611s carried a crew of two, a driver and a medical orderly. No turret was fitted to the FV611 although the Army did convert some APCs into ambulances for duty in Northern Ireland. These retained the turret. A roof extension was added to the rear of a small number of converted ambulances. This was to facilitate the use of the gravity-fed blood transfusion equipment to the patient in the upper stretcher.

Kremlin 1 and Kremlin 2 Internal Security Vehicles

The Russian word 'Kremlin' simply means fortress and this is what these internal security Saracens were. They were conversions of existing models, either the Mk2 or Mk3 Saracen (normal or RFC, respectively) but fitted with appliqué armour and vision blocks. The Kremlin 2 was for, to quote official documents, 'additional security requirements'.

Estimates of how many Saracens of all types were built vary between 1,049 and 1,838. An oddly coincidental number, 603, went to the British Army and the remainder went abroad. In 1963 it was replaced for front-line work in the British Army by GKN Sankey's FV432 tracked APC and later by the Alvis-made FV103 Spartan tracked APC, but it was retained in service until at least 1983 for internal security work.

BUILDING A SARACEN

All the FV600 series of fighting vehicles were built along the same principles, although there were notable differences in the superstructures. Here is a description of how the Saracen was made, and of Alvis's Fighting Vehicle Department.

The Factory

The Fighting Vehicle Department was an extension at the rear of the aero engine factory on the Holyhead Road and covered an area of 110,000sq. ft (10,200 sq.m) in two equal bays. One bay, the fabrication area, was covered by a 5-ton overhead pendant controlled crane. It was built on the City side of the Alvis Bridge in late 1950 as a replacement for the original Alvis factory, which had been destroyed in the Blitz in November 1940.

The site sloped from the Holyhead Road, at the front of the site, to the River Sherbourne at the rear. The Fighting Vehicle shop floor was at the Holyhead Road level. As a consequence there was a basement area beneath the shop floor of an equal size and this was invaluable as an FV stores area. Components were put together in suitable batch sizes and transferred to the production staging areas by a lift.

The Building Process

Stage 1: Cutting Out

The first stage in production was to cut the armour plate into the shapes required to make up the hull on a longitudinal flame profiler (oxyacetylene). The shapes were derived from steel templates being followed be a powered, knurled, magnetized roller. Some marking out was carried out in this area, to establish centrelines for subsequent operations. Plate edges were dressed to remove the scale from profiling.

Stage 2: Hull Build

This was carried out on a main-build fixture mounted on two large horizontal rotating manipulators and one static-build stand for the top half of the hull. The bottom half of the hull was fabricated on the first rotating fixture whilst the top half of the hull was being built on the static-build fixture. The two halves of the hull were then put together on the second manipulator and the welding completed. The second manipulator provided full access to the interior of the hull, whereas the first manipulator carried the location frames for the hull structure.

One of the two massive rotating manipulators that hold the main build fixtures that enable the two-stage process of welding the hull. This manipulator is used for the first part of the operation, where the lower half of the hull is welded. (Roland Andrews)

In this picture, actually of a Saladin, the final welding of the hull is taking place. (Roland Andrews)

Hull boring, where the holes to take the drive shafts are drilled. The massive piece of apparatus on the right drills through both sides of the hull, using the guides that can be seen adjacent to the wheel stations. (Roland Andrews)

With the hull bored, the smaller holes for the bolts that secure the suspension stations to the hull are drilled. (Roland Andrews)

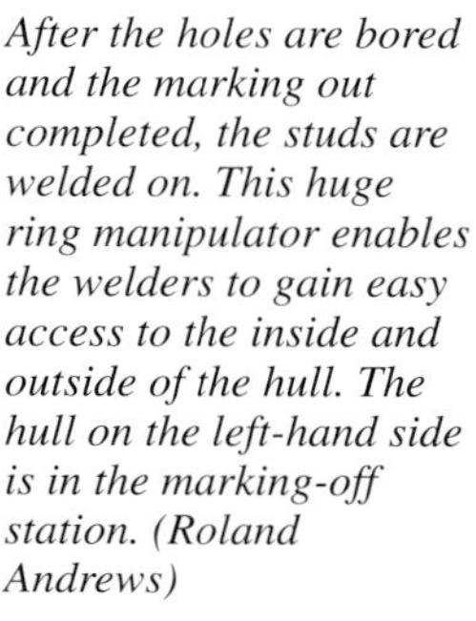

After the holes are bored and the marking out completed, the studs are welded on. This huge ring manipulator enables the welders to gain easy access to the inside and outside of the hull. The hull on the left-hand side is in the marking-off station. (Roland Andrews)

The fabrication area, where such operations as the fitting and welding of the nosepiece and other bolt- and weld-on hull components were fitted. Here also the Aralditing of the wheel stations took place. (Roland Andrews)

Stage 3: Wheel Station Bevel Box Housings

At this stage the wheel station bevel box housings were welded to the hull at the six locations provided by the access holes in the hull side plates.

Stage 4: Hull Boring

The transmission centrelines were established by boring the bevel box housings in line in a fixture mounted integrally with a horizontal-boring machine. A boring bar was used to bore each pair of transmission bores across the hull. The fixture determined the accurate pitch of the bores at the other wheel stations. Remembering that the sides of all FV600s were not perpendicular, but at an angle to the vertical. Drilling these holes accurately through the thick armour plate was crucial.

Stage 5: Hull Drilling

With the transmission bores established, the hull was then drilled using horizontal drilling machines located either side of the hull, the hole positions being determined by fixtures locating in the machined bores on the hull.

Stage 6: Marking Off

From the machined bores, transmission centrelines were established for the location of studs and bosses and welded components whose position is critical to the transmission bores, namely gearbox and engine mountings. In order to relieve an overloaded jig and tool department, Vauxhall Motors were given a contract to design the location fixtures for the groups of studs and bosses on the hull. Production Manager Roland Andrews visited Vauxhall several times during this exercise and what he saw confirmed his views on the merits of flow-line production.

Stage 7: Stud Welding

In this operation studs and bosses were welded to the hull structure using the drawn-arc stud welding process. This is a fully automatic process where the stud or boss is held in close contact with the plate by the welding gun and when the trigger is pressed, an arc is drawn between the stud and the plate. At the end of the weld cycle the stud is returned to the plate. The weld cycle time, depending on the size of the stud, is in the order of three-fifths of a second. Studs or bosses up to 3/4in can be welded by this method. In order to facilitate welding in the down-hand position the hull is mounted in a rotating ring-type manipulator.

The final build line where, on an elevated track, the suspension, the wheel stations, the engine, transmission and drive line, and the interior components are fitted to the painted hull. Work in progress would take several weeks, with an average of one completed vehicle per week coming off the tracks. (Roland Andrews)

All the mechanical components were sub-assembled before transferring to the final build line. Here is the steering sub-assembly section. (Roland Andrews)

Stage 8: Detail Components – Fitting and Welding

At a floor station and using a ring manipulator, detail components such as bulkhead mounting brackets, visor flaps, and torsion bar mounting brackets were fitted and welded to the hull.

Stage 9: Aralditing Wheel Stations

In order to provide a flat surface to mount the suspension brackets to the hull, a layer of two-pack epoxy cold-setting filler was used as a gasket between the brackets and the hull side plates. This was achieved with the aid of a fixture carrying the link brackets, locating from the flange face of the bevel box housing bored and faced at Stage 3. The contact surface on the armour plate was prepared by surface grinding. A thick layer of epoxy filler was applied and, with the fixture in place, the link brackets were bolted to the sideplate. A paper gasket was used to prevent adhesion to the link brackets by the epoxy filler. This technique was to save an expensive machining operation at each wheel station on the hull.

Stage 10: Fitting and Welding

At floor stations on a floor-mounted roller track, the nosepiece, engine louvres, side escape hatches, driver's visor and side visors, and the rear doors were fitted, completing the hull structure. Following this stage the hull was transferred to the paint station on a trolley fixture to facilitate movement in and out of the paint booth and the drying room.

The paint system on a ferrous armoured vehicle such as Saladin and Saracen consisted of a red-oxide priming coat, a battleship-grey undercoat and one intermediate coat of olive gloss (weather protection) followed by several coats of olive drab, the final paint coat being applied after vehicle road test. Some of the paint coats had protracted drying times, up to twenty-four hours, so there were several hulls in work in the paint area at any one time.

Stages 11, 12 13 and 14: Vehicle Build

These stages were completed progressively on an elevated roller track. Stage 11 was the installation of the main electric and plumbing systems in the bare hull. On Stages 11 and 12, on the outside of the vehicle, the suspension and wheel station assemblies and so on were fitted, whilst on the inside of the hull the gearbox, steering, transmission components and fuel tank and so on were mounted.

With road wheels fitted the vehicle was rolled down a ramp onto the wheels. At Stage 13 the engine radiator and twin cooling fans were fitted and the vehicle fuelled and prepared for road test. The final build line had fitting areas on both sides for the sub-assembly of wheel stations, transfer box, suspension components and the preparation of the engine prior to installation into the vehicle.

The Ministry of Defence funded plant and equipment for Saracen production. This covered machine tools and welding equipment down to powered hand tools leased to the company on an annual rental basis and only changed in 1960 when Roland Andrews, the Production Supervisor, wanting replacement equipment, found that no provision had been made for depreciation because of the leasing arrangement.

Road Test

Saracen being a wheeled rather than a tracked vehicle, it was permissible to test the vehicle on the roads in and around Coventry. The test programme was for a minimum of 100 miles (160km), 50 miles (80km) running in at limited speeds and 50 miles of performance testing. The only serious problem experienced, initially, was the wear of the Bendix couplings (between the Tracta forks in the transmission) due to severe tip loading. They would weld themselves together and then tear the weld apart. This would occur very early on the test programme. The test crews referred to the sound of the surfaces chafing against each other as 'dogs barking', as this was exactly what the sound was like as the joints rotated. This was overcome by

A Saracen after taking its first partially submerged test in a river. Contemporary reports say it was a lot more difficult getting out up the slippery bank that it was getting in! (Roland Andrews)

packing the joints with graphite grease and lowering the suspension to provide a level drive-coupling (as if the vehicle was fully laden). Once the joints were run in there was no further problem.

Transmission wind up was only a problem on metalled roads and flat surfaces. On cross-country the road wheel oscillation relieved any wind up. Andrews was telephoned by the police one morning who complained that one of the Saracens going up the Holyhead Road was seen to be driving with the nearside wheels on the kerb. The test driver was Ronald 'Soapy' Sutton who had joined Alvis after a spell with Jaguar, where amongst much other test work he had driven a slightly modified XK120 sports car in a record breaking run at 132mph (212km/h) along the Jabekke highway in Belgium. The introvert Sutton, always totally absorbed in his work, explained that driving the Saracen with the wheels on the kerb and going over the carriage crossings was a good way to relieve transmission wind up.

5 The Salamander

'The purpose of the vehicle is: 1. Saving life from crashed aircraft, and 2, Isolating and extinguishing fires in crashed aircraft.' The RAF service manual for the Alvis FV651/652 Salamander fire crash tender could not state its own priorities, and those of all firefighting services, more clearly. The saving of life is the most important function.

In flying, the most likely times that a crash will occur are during take-off and landing. And with a large load of fuel, the danger from fire is ever present. The last years of the Second World War saw the introduction of the jet aircraft into active service. With jets came new fuels, creating the likelihood of far more catastrophic results from a crash, and the faster take-off and landing speeds meant that an aircraft could easily overshoot and crash beyond the airfield perimeter. With the intense heat that can be generated in an aircraft fire and the entrapment of the occupants in an enclosed space, speed in getting to a crash is vital. Survival in a crashed plane is reckoned to depend on isolating the occupants within three minutes of the outbreak of fire. When a plane has crashed beyond an airfield perimeter, this time limit brings the need for a vehicle with rapid response capabilities into sharp focus.

NEW VEHICLES FOR OLD

The medium for fighting fires had been under scrutiny by an Air Ministry Technical Panel since 1944 and they decided that the best method was first to shoot foam in large quantities, supported by carbon dioxide (CO_2). In 1949, evaluating their requirement for fire cover for 1952 and beyond, the RAF considered that the existing 3-ton Austin K6 fire crash tenders could not carry the equipment essential for the job. The plan then was to commission a new 3-ton with the necessary equipment and a 10-ton vehicle as a reserve. In November 1950 the proposed categories of fire appliances in RAF stations were decided as: a) a heavy fire crash tender; b) a medium fire crash tender; and c) a domestic fire tender, the latter not being required on flying stations where the other two were deployed. During the war, quarter-ton jeep quick-response fire tenders were used, but it was felt by some, but by no means all involved, that the job done by a quarter-ton vehicle would be served by the new heavy crash tender. The role of a small rapid intervention vehicle generated an argument that would run on.

Further, the deployment, or establishment, to use the official RAF terminology, would depend on the nature of the aircraft flown from the stations. Due for introduction in 1954 in the RAF were the Hawker Hunter fighter and the English Electric Canberra and Vickers Valiant bombers, all jets. On the horizon were the Gloster Javelin night and all-weather fighter, the supersonic English Electric Lightning fighter, the Handley Page Victor and Avro Vulcan bombers and a new jet trainer, the Hunting Aviation Jet Provost. The plan in the early 1950s was that where jets or four-engined aircraft, either piston or turboprop, were based, the station would have two medium and two heavy fire crash tenders, the heavy vehicle using a new fire-fighting medium, foam. Where all other types were flown there would be one

The RAF Fire Service

The need for rapid response to a crashed plane on an airfield was understood from the early days of aviation. From 1912 until 1918, Britain's military flying was carried out by the Royal Naval Air Service and the Royal Flying Corps. As a part of the Army, the RFC followed the Army's firefighting code and the airfields were equipped with handcarts with water tanks and hoses to get to planes that crashed on landing. These aircraft landed in a very short distance on small fields and the fire crews, made up from the men serving on the base, could reach them almost as quickly as it took to hand-start a motor vehicle. Even so, a 'flamer' could engulf the simple wood and linen structures of these early planes extremely quickly.

But aviation development accelerated at a pace its pioneers never imagined. Equipped with two, three or more engines, planes flew faster, got bigger, carried ever more people and needed more fuel. With this came a greater potential danger to the occupants and this manifested itself in some major accidents in the early 1920s.

The first dedicated firefighting unit was started at the RAF Motor Transport Depot at Shrewsbury and, very soon after, firefighting instructors were trained at RAF Cranwell under Captain Desborough. Early RAF fire-fighting vehicles were based on the surviving Crossley tenders and Model T Fords from the Great War, but in the 1930s new Crossley and Morris chassis were ordered, followed by the Karrier Bantam and the Fordson WOT1. The most distinctive of the inter-war RAF fire-fighting vehicles was the Crossley P Type with a teardrop-shaped body, designed so that it would be easily cleaned after a gas attack.

In 1940 the Fire Training School moved to RAF Weeton near Blackpool, but three years later it moved again. This time its home was at Sutton-on-Hull where, under Squadron Leader Booker MBE, it was renamed the RAF School of Firefighting. A new rank of Firefighter (later changed to Fireman) was created and the school gained yet another new name, the RAF School of Firefighting and Anti-Gas.

Wartime vehicles continued to be a mixture of types. Added to the existing Fordson WOT1s were 2×4 Austin K2s and 4×6 Austin K6s, some of the latter being fitted out as gas trucks. The K6 was very much an RAF vehicle. It was used in many guises such as a crew bus, a mobile recruiting office and a GS lorry. Also used were some American 1½-ton Chevrolets, a weight class by then virtually obsolete within the US military, which were supplied under Lend-Lease. Jeeps were also used as fast rescue tenders.

In November 1953 the newly crowned Queen Elizabeth II presented the Fire Fighting School, represented by Air Marshall Sir Victor E. Groom KCVO KBE CBE DFC with new colours, bearing the motto *E Flammis Atque Ruinis Sallus* – 'Safety from Flames and Ruin'.

The lessons learnt from the war were gradually shaping all of Britain's Armed Forces. 1953 saw the introduction of the first fire crash truck, the Thorneycroft 4×4, designated by the RAF as the Mk5. There had been no previous specific designations of this mark; curious as there were at least five different vehicle types procured previously. From 1958 the Mk6 Salamander came into service, backed up by Thorneycroft DP (Dual-Purpose) vehicles and Land Rover Aircraft Crash Rescue Trucks (ACRT), using dry foam. The one-ton Austin $C0_2$ vehicle, as envisaged by the RAF, did not materialize for the reason that the K9 chassis used by the Army in the early 1950s was no longer in production.

1960 saw the inauguration of the Armed Forces Defence Fire Service (AFDFS) at RAF Manston near Ramsgate, Kent. The service was civilianized to a great degree, although some two thirds of the firefighters serving the RAF were RAF personnel so as not to compromise security at overseas bases. By 1976 the RAF Fire Service was incorporated into the Security Trade Group, although RAF Regiment officers retained responsibility for personnel. At that time the RAF School of Firefighting moved in with the AFDFS at Manston. It is of note that in the 1970s all defence firefighting vehicles were painted olive drab and the Mk6 was no exception.

As time progressed the Mk6 was replaced by successive mark numbers, the latest being the Mk10, Mk11 and the Mk12. The current Major Foam Vehicle (MFV) has recently been joined in service by another Alvis product, the Rapid Intervention Vehicle (RIV).

The author is grateful to Steven Shirley and Brian Harris of the Fire Museum, Manston, Kent, for providing information and photographs relating to the RAF Mk6/6A, and information on firefighting in the RAF in general.

medium and one heavy fire crash tender and where just light aircraft were flown a single medium crash tender would be established. Non-flying stations would have domestic fire appliances, as there would be no special requirements.

The need for enhanced fire cover was pressing and thus, as an interim measure, the Thornycroft Mk5 heavy fire crash tender was introduced into service. The Mk5 was a conventional 4×4 truck of wartime design, powered by a Rolls-Royce B80 petrol engine and carrying 400gal (1,800ltr) of water plus foam compound, but it was not a fast vehicle nor, because of its narrow track and high centre of gravity, a stable performer off-road. Clearly, there was an urgent need for a fire crash tender that was faster and more capable than the Thornycroft. In addition, the number of fire crash tenders had declined whilst the requirement for them had grown, thus the imperative was on numbers as well as performance. The Mk5 was supplemented and eventually replaced by the Mk5A, a much improved version, but the need was for something better than this, so the Directorate of Supply, Research and Development requested the Chief Engineer of the Fighting Vehicle Research and Development Establishment to come up with it. Competitive trials were held in the summer of 1953 and Alvis took their Saracen to the party.

GENESIS OF THE SALAMANDER

Tracked vehicles were among the entrants in the trials, but it was wheeled vehicles the MoS liked best. These were faster, more manoeuvrable and did no damage to the runways. Especially, they liked the performance of the Saracen. The type of ground surrounding an airfield could be rough or boggy and the FV600's independent suspension could cope with a great variety of going. The Ministry of Supply were eager for the new vehicle, for in January 1954 they indicated to Alvis that an FV600 variant would appear to be, with suitable engine and wheel modifications, what they wanted. There was, the MoS thought, a potentially large market for a specialized fire crash tender: they suggested

The Salamander hull, with its rear-mounted radiator. The extreme forward control position is clearly shown. The vertical steering column carried the gear selector, close to the driver's left hand. The lever on the floor is for the transfer case. The tube adjacent to the nearside front wheel is the fuel filler. (Roland Andrews)

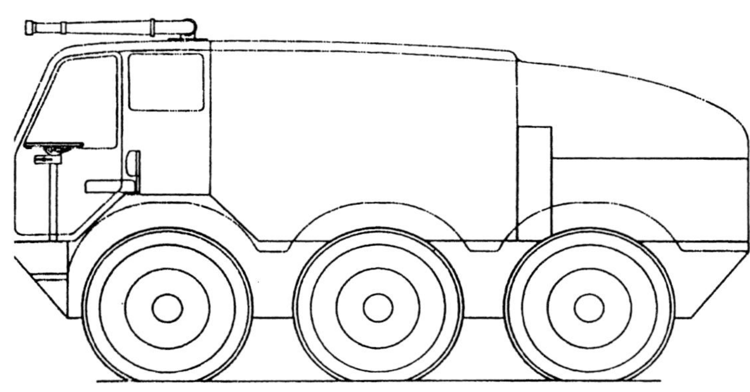

An outline drawing of the proposed Mk6 body, or 'top hamper' as firefighters refer to it. (Manston Fire Museum)

that the RAF would need about 500, and that civil aviation authorities would express a great interest.

In the light of the fact that there could be private sales, the question of funding the development of the new vehicle arose. The MoS came to an agreement with Alvis that it should be funded jointly as a semi-private venture. Rolls-Royce, as makers of the engine, would also contribute some development costs to the project.

The MoS gave the project the designation FV6001 and Alvis built a preliminary vehicle. Experience with the Saracen had suggested that a number of variants might be developed and given different numbers. Thus, to avoid confusion between these possible variants, a generic name, alliterative to those of the FV6001's family members, was sought. The vehicle was named Salamander after the mythical ancient Greek creature that could live in fire.

Although it was a Saracen that won over the minds of the men from the Ministry, it was the rear-engine layout of the FV601 Saladin that was used. In the drawing office, Fred Philips laid out the running gear in the new all-welded hull, placing the radiator behind the engine. The engine was mated to the centrally mounted pre-selector gearbox. This box was not the MoD's first choice: they envisaged a full automatic transmission. However, they accepted the pre-selector for the time being.

Although not armoured, FV6001 would be heavier than its FV600 predecessors – it was to carry 700gal (3,180ltr) of water, which alone weighed over 3 tons, and 100gal (455ltr) of foam compound. Speed, and more particularly acceleration, was of prime importance so more power was needed. The hull was fitted out with a 6.52 litre Rolls-Royce B81 Mk8, an overbored version of the B80. Even this would not deliver the right power curve, but until Rolls-Royce had developed an uprated version it would suffice for the preliminary vehicle.

As the FV6001 was not a fighting vehicle, it did not need the low profile crucial in presenting a difficult target to an enemy. Indeed a high forward-control driving position was necessary for good visibility and maximum use of load space. Thus the driver was seated on top of the chassis at the very front. A vertically mounted steering column was placed in the centre of the front of the vehicle. The MoS had contracted Pyrene in Brentford, Middlesex, to design and build the body and equip it with firefighting equipment. They produced a basic, boxy body for the first preliminary vehicle that was acceptable for the tests, in time for it to be displayed at the 1954 Military Vehicle Exhibition at Chertsey.

The Ministry of Supply cleared the vehicle for testing by the end of March 1955 and it was dispatched to the FVRDE at Cobham. Problems were to be expected in such a new type of vehicle. It was fitted with tanks and ballast to represent the weight of its equipment, but that weight with driver, but

The first preliminary vehicle, FV6001, with a very basic body by Pyrene, Note the forward-hinged doors. (Martin Wickham)

no crew, was only 7½cwt (380kg) – less than the maximum that the suspension could handle. This was inadequate to accommodate the weight of the other five crew members, assuming a weight of 12 stone (76kg) per man.

The vehicle proved difficult to drive. The driver's seat was uncomfortable and the accelerator pedal too high for comfort during prolonged use. The power-steering valve was not of a suitable type, causing a disconcerting chatter in the steering when the wheels were turned sharply at speed. The crew were not provided with any grab handles, making it difficult to ride in when driven at speed off-road and putting them in danger in an emergency stop. As suspected, the torsion bars of the suspension were not up to the weight, restricting the vehicle to a speed of 12mph (19km/h) during the mere 17 miles (27km) that it was run over the suspension course. The testers were able to run the FV6001 over 3,708 miles (5,967km) on other surfaces such as the test track and hard roads, but the vehicle was returned to Alvis with the tests not fully complete.

However, the MoS had confidence in Alvis's ability to put the problems right. The vehicle would be put out to tender according to correct procedure but, by the following January, the MoS gave verbal notification of a contract, worth £40,000, for forty chassis which were scheduled, rather optimistically, for delivery between January and June of 1956. Alvis fitted the modifications required to a second chassis, numbered FV651. The gearbox was not the full automatic the FVRDE had wanted, but the five-speed pre-selector. The single range forward-and-reverse transfer box was strengthened to take the extra load and fitted with a power take-off to drive the pumps. Rolls-Royce had a new engine ready too, the B81 Mk8A. To produce the right power curve it had a high-compression cylinder head, requiring it to run on 98-octane petrol and producing 235bhp at 4000rpm, 250rpm higher than previous B80/81 engines had been governed. Torque was raised to 314lb/ft at 2,700rpm, and these figures meant the Mk8A was the most powerful B-series variant made.

Pyrene had completed their design for the production body and this was fitted to the second preliminary vehicle. Now that the suspension had been uprated to cope with the extra weight and all the recommended modifications to the chassis had been made, trials of the second vehicle began at Cobham in August 1956. These were completed by the end of the following December. The crew accommodation was much improved, being described by the testers as having a high degree of comfort. The GVW of the vehicle was now 12.6 tons (12,800kg). There were some problems with the second prototype, as would be expected, but most of them were no more than teething troubles. However, at first the engine had a tendency to overheat and burn out the exhaust valves. The design of the B81 engine itself did little to help this. To allow for the bigger bore size the cylinders were siamesed, allowing no space for cooling water between pairs. Nor did the octane rating of the fuel available help, as its tetra-ethyl lead content was too low for the Mk8A engine's high compression, aggravating the overheating. Cooling trials would continue in the hands of General Fire Appliances in late 1957. The preliminary vehicle had foam apparatus fitted and this was tested at the RAF station at Moreton-in-Marsh. A major concern to the testers was that the body and equipment was on top of the transmission, which made major maintenance a very lengthy process. Even suspension maintenance was difficult with the depth of bodywork.

Initially Alvis had a great deal of work on with the Saracen and so had decided to subcontract the chassis. However, the subcontractors were not fabricating the chassis well, so Alvis brought the job in-house. Alvis's production engineer, Roland Andrews, introduced the very first semi-automatic thin-wire CO_2 welding method recently developed in the USA. The complete chassis, fitted with a front panel by Coventry Sheet Metal, was driven down to Pyrene, either by Alvis or Pyrene drivers, where the body and equipment was installed. The firefighting media were water, foam and Chlorobromodifluormethane (CBM). From Pyrene, each was delivered to RAF Cosford from where they were despatched to one of five RAF Commands: Fighter, Bomber, Coastal, Flying Training or Transport. Each had its own pool of vehicles and from these the individual vehicles were dispatched to the stations that required them.

Delivery of FV651 chassis was held up by Rolls-Royce, who could not supply enough engines in time. Whilst no record seems to be

The second preliminary vehicle, with the finalized design of production body.The doors are now hinged at the rear, making for a safer exit at the scene of an emergency. The brush guard would not be fitted to production vehicles. This vehicle was tested by the FVRDE, supposedly to destruction. Whatever condition it was in, in February 1968 it was officially transferred to the RAF who sold it out of service a year later. (Manston Fire Museum)

available as to the nature of the problem it may be that they were trying to cure the overheating. Of the forty vehicles due for delivery, it was then believed that only a small number were likely to be finished by the end of 1956. In reality only one vehicle was finished by that time, as testing still continued with the FVRDE. Ongoing problems meant that the first twenty-seven would be sent back and forth between the RAF, Pyrene and Alvis until they were up to standard. It would be towards the end of 1958 before all forty vehicles were delivered. In September 1958, as delivery of the FV651 was virtually complete, an RAF memo was issued, outlining the vehicle requirements for improved firefighting facilities. These would be for:

- **Truck, Fire Crash, GP**: A fire truck for airfield duty having a very high firefighting potential with a high degree of mobility
- **Truck, Water, Fire Crash DP**: A dual-purpose water truck used primarily to support the Truck, Fire Crash GP. May also be used for domestic firefighting
- **Truck, Water, Fire Domestic**: A fire truck for general firefighting and to satisfy the special requirements of large hutted stations and certain MUs.

The 'Truck, Fire Crash, GP' would be either the FV651 Salamander, which the RAF would number as the Mk6, or the Thorneycroft Mk5 or latterly Mk5A. Because of the delays in delivery the Mk6 would be allocated on a priority basis. Even then, there was a serious shortfall in the numbers of top-line vehicles and already demands were being made for a further forty-eight Mk6s to bring the establishment up to full strength.

The 'Truck, Fire Crash', in practice a foam vehicle, either a Mk5, Mk5A or a Mk6, would work as part of a team of vehicles, including Land Rover Aircraft Crash Recovery Tenders (ACRTs) and Dual-Purpose (DP) tenders. The ACRT would usually be first to the scene, to isolate the part of the aircraft that contained personnel. As soon as the fire was under control the crews would then be able to move in to rescue the occupants. A foam vehicle would follow immediately to contain and

The first production version of the FV651 Salamander, the Mk6, pictured at the rear of Alvis's Coventry factory. Note the foam hoses in the locker between the front and centre wheels, the centrally placed steering wheel and just below it the lever for the pre-selector gearbox. The CBM hoses are stored on a reel above the rear wheel. Later models would have the CBM hoses in the same location, but in a cage. (Roland Andrews)

Salamanders at various stages of construction, the furthest advanced is fitted with the body front. In this form it was driven to Pyrene in West London. (Roland Andrews)

extinguish the fire. The Mk6's speed and its cross-country ability were its major assets. It could travel at over 60mph (97km/h) on the runway, which was a phenomenal speed considering that heavy lorries of the day had been restricted to 20mph (32km/h) on public roads. This speed meant that the Mk6 had the ability to arrive at an incident within the crucial three minutes. Following behind the ACRTs the foam vehicle crew's duty was to extinguish the fire with foam from the monitor and with water. Following the foam vehicle would be the DP vehicles, providing more medium as the foam vehicle's tanks were run down.

ESTABLISHMENT

The first three of the original order of forty FV651s off the production line were earmarked as driver training vehicles, going into service in 1957 at the RAF School of Fire Fighting and Rescue at Sutton-on-Hull for aerodrome/crew training. Two of these were planned for redeployment at the RAF Flying College, Manby and at RAF Syreston, after the training for the new vehicle and the deployment of the rest of the order was completed, leaving one at Sutton-on-Hull for training replacement crews. The remaining thirty-seven went to front-line RAF stations where jet and multi-engined propeller aircraft were in use, such as Coningsby, St Mawgan, Scampton and Tangmere. Three vehicles would go overseas. One would go to Nicosia, Cyprus, where EOKA terrorists were causing trouble during the progress to the island's independence. Another went to Khormaksar in Aden Protectorate, where the RAF was maintaining Support and Communications Squadrons for the Army during the rebellion there. The third went to Changi, Singapore, where transport planes and helicopters were maintained in support of the ongoing Malayan crisis (*see* chapters 3 and 9). A second batch of four was requested for reserve at Fighter Command Ready-for-Use Pool, but did not materialize at this time.

G19 – THE RCAF'S SALAMANDER

From the time the FV6001 was displayed at Chertsey it was generating overseas interest. In late 1954, Col. Chaylor of Alvis's sales team met with representatives from the Royal Canadian Air Force, who had very much liked what they saw. In

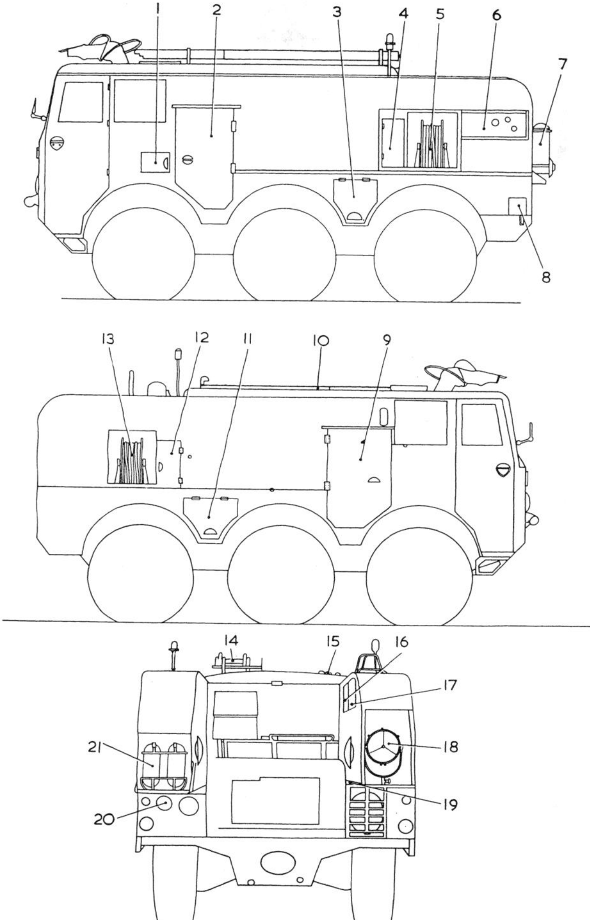

Mk6 Equipment Stowage Positions.
1 No. 11 Locker: Fuel tank filler
2 No. 10 Locker: Foam sidelines
3 No. 9 Locker: Pump suction valve and connection
4 No. 8 Locker: CO_2 cylinders, chassis system
5 CBM Hose and applicators
6 CBM Control panel
7 Power pack for pneumatic circular saw
8 Pneumatic circular saw machine
9 No. 1 Locker: Foam sidelines
10 Crowbar, salving hook
11 No. 2 Locker: Foam compound replenishment pump
12 No. 3 Locker: Water tank pressure refilling connection
13 CBM Hose and applicator
14 Extending ladder
15 Crowbar, saving hook
16 No. 6 Locker: Compound pickup tube
17 No. 5 Locker: Floodlight cable reel
18 No. 4 Locker: Floodlight
19 Tripod for main floodlight
20 Mains snatchplug socket
21 Power pack for pneumatic saw

the early 1950s the RCAF had been using a version of the RAF Thorneycroft Mk5, which they numbered as the G21. The RCAF version was fitted with a foam monitor at the rear of the vehicle. It was the Salamander's cross-country ability, its higher water and foam capacity, and a foam monitor that was operated through a hatch in the cab roof that attracted the RCAF. They would be interested in buying the FV651 on a private basis rather than through the Ministry of Supply and soon a Canadian firm, the Four Wheel Drive Auto Company Ltd, was lined up to act as agents for Alvis. But the RCAF was not prepared to pay the £18,550 asking price for each chassis. This was considerably more than the £8,500 that the Ministry of Supply were paying for complete vehicles, but the MoS had paid for a significant proportion of the development, thus on delivery the MoS were in effect paying the manufacturing costs. Alvis then agreed to ship the chassis to Canada at Rolls-Royce's and their joint expense.

Initially, the Four Wheel Drive Company was to arrange for a body to be supplied locally. John Parkes had already discussed with the American fire appliance manufacturer, American LaFrance, the idea of building a body on a chassis that would

The prototype FV651 that was sent to Canada for winter trials. (Pat Ware)

A fleet of Salamanders lined up outside Pyrene's factory on the Great West Road in Brentford, Middlesex. These vehicles, identified by the absence of CBM hoses, are destined for the RCAF. (Manston Fire Museum)

be paid for by the MoS on chassis shipped out to the USA. Nothing would come of any arrangements to make a body for the Salamander in either the USA or Canada, but an FV651 chassis with a well-built Pyrene cab and a large ballast weight was sent for trials to the RCAF station at Rockcliffe, Ottawa, in early 1956. Ron Walton, whose work was so vital to the Saracen development, was sent out to sort out some problems that the Canadians were having with the vehicle. In deep snow and ice he discovered and rectified some carburettor icing problems that had severely hampered the top speed of the vehicle. Incidentally, some two and a half years later via Tecalemit (Foamite) Ltd of Canada, US fire truck manufacturers American LaFrance contacted Alvis. Some representatives of the US Navy had seen the FV651 demonstration in Ottawa and were interested in it. No further developments were understood to have come of this either.

An RCAF G19. As well as the larger driving mirrors, there are other differences between the G19 and the Mk6. Note the different monitor, or turret nozzle, as the RCAF termed it. This was a modification of the original Pyrene item, fitted as a result of a recommendation by RCAF driver/instructor Ian Morrison. The bright metal extension was simply screwed on to the original Pyrene nozzle barrel. Note also that there are no BCF hoses, as the RCAF did not have a requirement for this medium. One of the compartments where the RAF's hoses would have been located was used to the house the Swingfire cab heater. (firehouse651.com)

A G19 of the RCAF in a training exercise. A crewman is operating the monitor through the roof hatch. (firehouse651.com)

In the event, the Canadian authorities ordered thirty-four vehicles at the end of 1956, the order coming to Alvis via the MoS through Pyrene. RCAF submitted a requirement to shoot foam on the move, circling the fire and shooting foam continuously if need demanded, so the PTO was redesigned to power the pump whilst the vehicle was moving. Alvis numbered this chassis variant as FV652. The G19's fitted equipment also differed from the RAF Mk6 in that the RCAF had no requirement for CBM nor for the air-powered tools on these vehicles. In March 1957, the RCAF enquired about seven FV652s for carrying dry powder, but in the event none were ordered.

Production problems, particularly with the delivery of the engine, meant that the Canadian order would be met in part out of the last ten of the forty chassis initially ordered by the MoS. These vehicles were dispatched from Pyrene's factory in early 1958, and entered service in the RCAF as the G19. About five went to RCAF airfields in England, France and Germany, with the rest staying in Canada. In September 1961 the RCAF expressed an interest in fifty more FV652s, but no more were ordered.

IN SERVICE WITH THE RCAF

Fighter Wings 1, 2, 3 and 4 of the RCAF went to Europe as part of the NATO defence force. Assembled first in November 1951 at RAF North Luffenham, Leicestershire, with No.1 Fighter Wing flying F86 Sabre aircraft, this was the largest ever RCAF fighter force. The RCAF established a British base at the former Second World War RAF Bomber Command station at Langar, near Nottingham, to serve as a supply depot for bases in Germany and France, which would be occupied by 1955. From 1958, fire cover by the G19 would be with RCAF No. 1 Wing at Grostenquin and No. 2 Wing at Metz, France, and with No. 3 Wing at Zweibrucken and No. 4 Wing at Baden-Soellingen in Germany. Fire cover was also provided by the RCAF for other NATO Air Forces using these bases.

Some of the RCAF's home bases were on front-line duty, as part of the NATO defence against a Soviet Union air attack that might come from over the Arctic. On these bases in winter the ambient temperatures could be as low as –40°F (–40°C).

As all fire tenders had to ready for action all the time that aircraft were either flying or on standby, operational procedures had to take the low temperatures into account. Tenders were kept in readiness in heated crash bays that prevented the water in the tanks from freezing and made the engines easy to start. G19 cabs were insulated with up to 1 3/4in of mineral wool and the vehicles fitted with a petrol-fired Swingfire cab heater.

Although it was a very effective firefighting tool and considered by some to be one of the best, if not the best fire crash truck in the RCAF, the G19 was not without its problems. The monitor, or the turret nozzle as the RCAF termed it, had four vane deflectors. These created a cone-shaped discharge that made if difficult for the turret operator to see the effect of his application. And when set to the straight-on position they had an adverse effect on the reach of the stream compared to a clean barrel. Driver/instructor Ian Morrison took the initiative to redesign the nozzle, fitting an upper and lower clamshell deflector that produced a flat, variable fan-shaped discharge and a clean discharge on straight stream. Canada's National Defence Headquarters worked on the idea, producing a single, flat upper-deflector that gave a better fan discharge. This was not a perfect solution, as the hydraulic effect when the device was engaged caused the turret to elevate with varying force, requiring a fair effort to control it, but it was a definite improvement.

The RCAF felt that the running gear was not up to the weight of the body and equipment, causing strain on the drivetrain. It spent a lot of time in the repair shops, earning the epithet of 'Hangar Queen'. A spare parts shortage, aggravated by the geographical distance, was a major contribution to the problem. The pre-selector gear box was not liked, being something of an unusual device on the North American continent. The regular practice of 'toggling up', the priming of the gearbox before driving to ensure that the bands were fully adjusted, was not always appreciated. Acting on behalf of Alvis, Pyrene in conjunction with the RCAF made a move to improve the performance by modifying or replacing the fluid flywheel and synchronizing

This single body was made by Pyrene's neighbours, Foamite. Although it was offered on both the Salamander and Thorneycroft Nubian Major chassis, it never went into production on the Salamander chassis. It seems, on appearance alone, to be of a much better standard of construction than the Pyrene body, which would suggest that it was more expensive. However, one of the reasons that it did not go into production, as pointed out by the then Flight Sergeant John Arthur to Foamite's people, was that the doors opened the wrong way and would slam on a crewmember's leg when he got out of the vehicle as it came to a stop. (Manston Fire Museum)

units. Eventually the powertrain in some, if not all of the G19s stationed in Canada was replaced with a Ford V8 engine and an Allison fully automatic gearbox. The G19's life in the RCAF in Canada was short: it and the G21 were replaced from 1964 by the Sicard MFV. This was a much larger 6×6 vehicle with greater foam capacity. The G19s operated at the RCAF's European bases were phased out from 1970.

SOUTH AFRICA AND CEYLON

In April 1959 Major Sullivan, Alvis's new sales manager, was asked to go to South Africa to follow up enquiries from the authorities there regarding the FV651, but it is not established as to whether any were actually delivered to South Africa.

A single FV652 was sent to the Royal Ceylon Air Force, but before it was dispatched it was exhibited at the 1959 Farnborough Air Show. This vehicle had a Pyrene body and, like the RCAF G19, was not fitted with CBM or BCF equipment. The RCYAF was a relatively new force, formed in 1950 after the country gained independence, although a number of RAF personnel were kept on secondment to assist in training before and after the formal hand-over in 1958. A small force, the RCYAF's main base was at Katunayeke, which, when renamed Nurango, was scheduled for expansion in the 1960s. The delivery of the vehicle, however, did not take place until after 1960 as there was, it seems, some delay in the hand-over procedure.

FV652 WITH THE RAF

The political situation in Britain had changed dramatically since 1954, when the Salamander was first conceived. The 1956 Suez Crisis signalled the end for Britain's role as a major world power. In 1957 the Conservative Government of the day produced a Defence Review White Paper, the content of which would have a significant impact on the RAF. With the loss of Empire the need to maintain air bases worldwide was under question and the threat of a nuclear attack by Russia, and Britain's defence and counter-attack capability, was thoroughly investigated. The White Paper's conclusions were that an enemy attack would be by Intercontinental Ballistic Missiles, which fighter aircraft would not be able to repel. Thus surface-to-air missiles, specifically the Bristol Bloodhound, would be deployed as a front-line defence. Fighter aircraft would be needed only to defend the V-bomber bases. In consequence, some of Fighter Command's British stations would be closed.

As the stations were closed, the equipment on them would naturally become surplus and this included a number of Mk5A fire crash tenders. The RAF liked the Mk6 and wanted more, but the Treasury were loathe to sanction the Air Ministry, which had taken over the responsibility of procuring equipment for the RAF after the Ministry of Supply was disbanded in 1959, to buy new ones at over £9,000 each. The Air Ministry, under pressure no doubt from Treasury, now considered that surplus Mk5As could be deployed in place of new Mk6s.

The decision about how many new Salamanders, if any, to buy was influenced by two other factors. The Mk6 was the heaviest fire crash tender yet to see service with the RAF, and although it could carry plenty of water and foam, its weight and width proved to be a fatal drawback – literally, in two instances. At RAF Oakington a plane crashed on the other side of a railway line to the airfield. The Land Rover ACRT got there first, being capable of struggling over the railway line, but the Mk6 could not cross the line to get to the scene quickly enough. Another serious incident occurred at RAF Cranwell, the officers' training college, where two aircraft collided on take-off. The planes landed in a field and the crash tenders used a narrow lane to reach the scene. The Mk6 slid into a ditch as the ground at the edge of the lane collapsed, blocking the path for the other vehicles. Again, only the Land Rover got to the incident in reasonable time.

A Mk6A, 03 AG 83. Note the 2,500gpm (11,365ltr/min) monitor and BCF hoses, flaked – that is, layered behind the grille above the rear wheel. This vehicle spent some time at RAF Biggin Hill. (Manston Fire Museum)

The question arose as to whether the expensive Mk6 was worth the money, when it had operational limits that could be sidestepped by a more economical change in operational procedure. A formula was worked out that assessed the Mk6's capability as being equal to that of two Mk5A's, a CO_2 truck and an ACRT combined. The argument was thus whether more Land Rovers at under £900 each should ordered, to work in tandem with the Mk5A, instead of ordering more Mk6s – erroneously understood, by some, to be costing £14,000 each (no RAF Salamander cost more than £10,500) – as some in the RAF had urged.

The idea would be to substitute the Mk6 with its equivalent four vehicles, the purchase of CO_2 trucks and ACRTs being cheaper and supposedly more versatile. However, with the extra crews required, these would be more expensive to man. The question of a Mk7, as yet only an idea, was again raised. Some found the wisdom of its original concept, as an 8×8, questionable and asked if the Mk6 could be upgraded in some form.

It was also believed that the gentle countryside surrounding some RAF stations rendered the Mk6's superb cross-country ability superfluous, and that Mk5As would be adequate to do the job. This argument was a powerful one that the RAF could not adequately counter. Like the RCAF's G19, the Mk6s suffered from a higher than normal degree of unserviceability. Some of this, in statistical form, was traced to the driver training establishments where, quite understandably, this new and complex vehicle was suffering at the hands of novices, and some of the down time was due to badly designed water and compound control valves. But some of the Mk6s at active stations were kept out of service by a shortage, or even a total lack of spare parts. This naturally had to be a factor in whether the numbers of Mk6s were added to or not.

Eventually it was decided to order more Mk6s, but estimates of the numbers the RAF would need varied between twenty and forty-eight. The newly formed Fire Services Committee, the part of the Air Ministry who had taken over that part of the procurement role from the now defunct Ministry of Supply, placed orders for more vehicles. The new model would be based on the FV652 chassis with a split PTO and would be numbered by the RAF as the Mk6A. Pyrene fitted a fibreglass foam tank in place of the original aluminium one and supplied bromochlorodifluoromethane (BCF) equipment in place of the CBM fitted to the Mk6s. The four reserve vehicles originally asked for in 1956 were finally delivered in 1960 and designated Mk6As, but in May 1959 the FSC had decided on twenty-

The British Army's Salamanders

One Salamander was issued to the British Army, and originally served at the ammunition dump at Kineton. The Army needed such a vehicle at Kineton, as it could traverse the earth mounds that had been built around the site to act as blast walls in the event of an explosion. This particular vehicle was fitted out as a water tender, with no foam capability, as water was the most suitable medium to put out ammunition fires. Ordered in January 1964, it was delivered in May 1965, it was operated by a civilian crew of the Army Fire Service.

The single Salamander sold to the British Army for use at the arms dump at Kineton. Note the different equipment carried. There is a ladder but no foam monitor – this vehicle was equipped with a single steel water tank. (Martin Wickham)

The Kineton vehicle from the front. Note the absence of a monitor, and the roof sign. (Manston Fire Museum)

The British Army's Salamanders (*cont.*)

The Kineton vehicle was converted to a water cannon and transferred to Northern Ireland as an Army vehicle for use in riot control situations. It is pictured here at the end of its service life, looking rather neglected. (Manston Fire Museum)

It remained at Kineton until 1971. It was then converted to a water cannon; a logical conversion, considering that a large water tank and a high-pressure pump were already in place. All it needed was a cannon, which was fitted. It was issued to the 17th/21st Lancers, for their tour of duty in Northern Ireland, for use in riot control. As the 17th/21st Lancers finished their tour of duty the vehicle remained in Northern Ireland and was transferred to the strength of other regiments when fulfilling their tours of duty. It was withdrawn from service in 1974, and sold out of service to a dealer in 1975.

five more. The order, actually for twenty-seven, was placed in June 1960 and delivery ran from October 1960 until late 1961. A third order, for nine, was placed in June 1961 and delivered between March and July 1963. This amounted to thirty-seven FV652s. In between these two last orders, three special driver-training vehicles, designated FV653, were built, fitted with a cab and no rear bodywork except for ballast tanks. They were delivered via Cosford to the No. 4 School of Mechanical Transport at St Athan, near Cardiff, in September 1962. These three vehicles would bring the total to eighty-three, less than half of the RAF's forecast for the 1963 requirement of 193 vehicles.

One of the three FV653s of the RAF No. 4 School of Mechanical Transport at St Athan with a ballast tank in place of the top hamper. Note the white wind-up markings painted on the hubs. The Driver Training vehicles were the only RAF Salamander versions to be thus marked. (Manston Fire Museum)

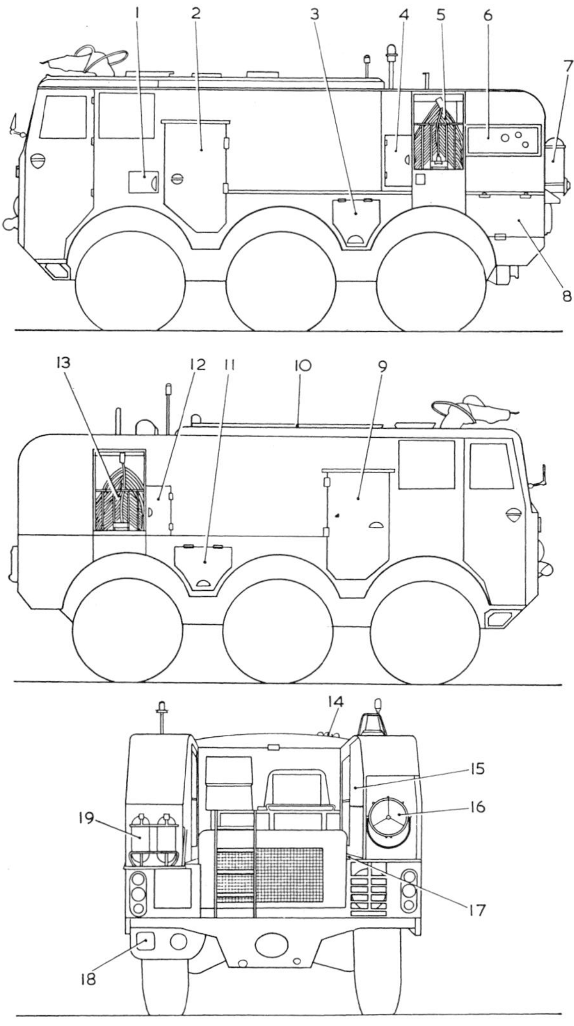

Mk6A Equipment Stowage Positions.
1 No. 11 Locker: Fuel tank filler
2 No. 10 Locker: Foam sidelines
3 No. 9 Locker: Pneumatic circular saw machine
4 No. 8 Locker: CO_2 cylinders, chassis system
5 BCF Hose and applicators
6 BCF Control panel
7 Power pack for pneumatic circular saw
8 Battery stowage
9 No. 1 Locker: Foam sidelines
10 Crowbar, salving hook
11 No. 2 Locker: Foam compound replenishment pump
12 No. 3 Locker: Water tank pressure refilling connection
13 BCF Hose and applicator
14 Crowbar, salving hook
15 No. 5 Locker: Floodlight cable reel
16 No. 4 Locker: Floodlight
17 Tripod for main floodlight
18 Mains snatchplug socket
19 Power pack for pneumatic saw

A NEW MONITOR

The RAF, like the RCAF, found that the 2,500gpm foam monitor was not as good as it should be. In critical circumstances it did not deliver as high a volume of foam as was needed. From 1962, new Mk6As would be delivered with a new two-position version that put out either 2,500gpm (11,365ltr/min) or 5,000gpm (22,730ltr/min). In addition, fifty of the vehicles already in service were retrospectively fitted with the new monitor by service personnel, a job estimated to take three days. However, RAF firefighters were in agreement with their Canadian counterparts that, in use, even the original monitor was 'a bit of a handful!'

MK6 IN OPERATION WITH THE RAF

For the whole time that aircraft were flying from an RAF airfield, the crew would be on duty, maintaining

Two Mk6Bs, which are upgrade Mk6s, at RAF Akrotiri in Cyprus. Note the CBM hoses on reels and the two-position monitor. The crew are wearing improved uniforms that were introduced in the mid-1960s. The two-piece suits, aluminized headgear and gloves give much better protection against the intense heat of an aviation spirit fire than the leather jerkins, denim fatigues, asbestos face masks and gloves that were worn up until then. (Manston Fire Museum)

and servicing their equipment, on standby to operate immediately if trouble was imminent. To ensure they were in proper working order, RAF firefighters would drive all their fire crash tenders every morning and evening around the perimeter track of the airfields on which they were stationed, in a prescribed 10-mile (16km) route. This routine had produced no problems for the previous models but, as the Salamander's drivetrain was inherited from the Saracen, there were two considerations to be taken into account. The suspension had been designed to cope with rough terrain and it needed to be 'exercised'

03 AG 83 in Mk6C form, with a larger two-position monitor. Note the flaked BCF hoses above the rear wheel. (Manston Fire Museum)

The Runway Friction Test Vehicle

Aircraft tyres don't do many road miles, but what work they have to do is very demanding. A bad landing can cause a blowout and result in disaster, so the tyres have to be built to a high standard of safety. As well as this, they have to handle braking on both dry and wet runways. To test aircraft tyres, the Road Research Laboratory in conjunction with the Ministry of Aviation asked Alvis to produce a runway friction test vehicle. Using a Salamander chassis, Alvis's design engineer, Alan Russell, set to work configuring an apparatus that fit within the vehicle. This equipment would mount an aircraft wheel in the centre of the vehicle and, when driven at speed, lower it onto the runway at varying loads and rates of descent. A full six-wheel drive configuration was thought unnecessary so the centre wheel stations were removed, and sufficient ballast fitted. The B81 engine was retained, although it is not now known whether the high-compression Mk8A or a dry-sump version of the low-comp Mk7 was used. However, to improve the maximum speed, the ratio of the hub reduction gears was altered. Alan Russell has fond memories of the project, describing it as an 'entertaining exercise'.

The Runway Friction Test vehicle, the only 4×4 FV600 variant ever made. The equipment for lowering the test wheel to the road can be seen under the vehicle. (Pat Ware)

through some degree of travel to ensure even distribution of grease in its suspension joints and to ensure that the Tracta joints were settled in correct alignment. The other was the business of driveline wind-up. Driving in the same direction every day, as had been the practice prior to the Salamander's introduction, would guarantee wind-up. Alvis's design engineer Alan Russell suggested to the RAF that the crews drove clockwise around the airfield on one day and anti-clockwise the next. This was too simple a solution for the bureaucrats who dismissed it as being 'against regulations'.

In practice, driveline wind-up was not the problem it was with the Saracen. Unless called to an incident, the 10-mile morning and evening runs was all the mileage they did, far less than that of a Saracen. And it was no problem at all to the crews to drive the route in one direction in the morning and the other in the evening. A bureaucrats' solution to the wind-up problem was that special free-running rollers should be built into the buildings that housed the vehicles, so that the wind-up could be driven out. In fact, very few buildings were fitted with the rollers. They were an unnecessary expense. An early remedy for the independent suspension 'exercise' tried by the RAF was to lay railway sleepers at short intervals along an out of the way part of the airfield. Later, on some airfields, permanent bumps, early versions of the speed bumps that now disfigure our city streets, were built.

The B81A's high-compression cylinder head demanded high-octane fuel, whereas the other vehicles in the fleet ran on a lower octane, as demanded by the FVDE when laying out the specifications for

The 8×8 Mk7

As early as 1950, even before a requirement for the Salamander was issued, its Mk7 replacement was under consideration. In 1958 the Ministry of Supply published a report, 'The Assessment of Future RAF Requirements for Fire Crash Tenders'. It recommended that three vehicles, carrying 500gal (2,273ltr), 750gal (3,410ltr) and 1,000gal (4,546ltr) of water respectively would meet those requirements. Although the Mk6 was criticized for its unreliability, its virtues of speed and cross-country performance were valued and much consideration was given to the use of its chassis components in the proposed vehicles. The main criticism of the Mk6 centred around the fact that too much was packed into too tight a space. Its suspension was working at its limits, and its transmission was overloaded, resulting in failures. In such a short-wheelbase vehicle the 700gal (3,410ltr) water tank was placed too high for stability and, when the vehicle required maintenance, accessibility to the drivetrain was difficult and time consuming.

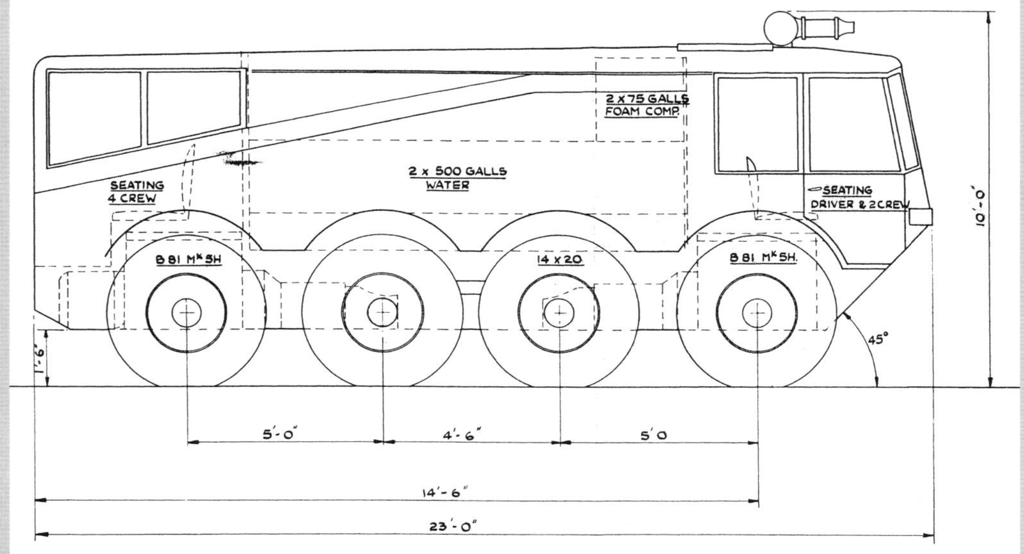

The FVRDE's drawing of the proposed 8×8 Mk7 fire crash tender, based on FV600 running gear. At 4ft 6in, the wheelbase between the second and third axle is shorter than the FV600's standard 5ft. Note the rear-facing seats for four of the crew. The outlines of the two engines, mounted front and rear, can be seen, as can the location of the water and foam tanks. No indication was given as to which of the eight wheels would steer. (REME Museum)

The report recommended that the 750gal (3,410ltr) vehicle requirement could be met by a completely new vehicle, as the additional weight would push the FV651s already stressed components beyond their limits, but the other categories could be met by vehicles based on FV651 components. The 500gal (2,273ltr) vehicle would effectively be a lightweight Salamander, using a new chassis of aluminium where possible, and the existing power train and suspension. This, combined with a smaller water tank would bring the weight down to 11$^{1}/_{2}$tons, which would be within the drivetrain and suspension components' working ability. Most interesting was the 1000gal (4,546ltr) vehicle. This would be an 8×8. It would weigh 16tons, have a wheelbase of 14ft 6in (4.42m) and be powered by two B81 engines. Whilst this monster would be the biggest firefighting vehicle the RAF had ever seen, the report considered that its greater size would counter the Mk6's shortcomings whilst still retaining its cross-country ability. There would be lower axle loadings and the water would be in two 500gal (2,273ltr) tanks stretched the length of the vehicle, reducing its centre of gravity and thus improving its stability. The engines would drive four wheels each, but only one engine would be used in light station duty. The transmissions would have less work to do, improving reliability. The layout could be greatly improved, making maintenance much better. And of course, using FV651 components, there would be a great degree of compatibility and a minimum of spares to be carried. But the Ministry of Supply had taken one bold step with the FV651 and the results had been less than ideal. The question of cost and the desire to play safe meant that future requirements would be met by conventional vehicles, the existing Mk5A and a new Mk7, which would be the Thorneycroft 6×6 Nubian Major.

all of the B-Series engines. This meant that separate fuel storage tanks had to be installed for the Mk6, adding to the expense of keeping the vehicles in service and likely turning some civil servants against the vehicle even more.

After around ten years' service each Mk6 would be sent to the workshops at RAF Leconfield, Yorkshire, where it would receive a total overhaul, the job taking approximately six months. They would then be returned to service, but almost always to a new home. The exception to this were two vehicles from the second batch of Mk6A/FV652s which, owing to the lateness of their delivery date, received no overhaul.

DECOMMISSIONING OF RAF MK6S

The Salamander was very much liked by some of its operators, who considered it to be the best they had used. However, it had its shortcomings. It was expensive to buy, had a degree of instability when driven at its limits, was difficult to maintain and its foam capacity was not as big as it could be. The forecast for the requirement of the vehicle worldwide for reserve and active service varied from 169 to 193, but these numbers were never realized, and surviving RAF records show that no more than eighty-three were bought. Although one vehicle was taken out of service in 1973, most decommissioning lasted from April 1975 to October 1977, which meant that the vehicle as a type was in service for nineteen years. It was replaced by the Thorneycroft Nubian Major, which would be designated as the Mk7, a conventional 6×6 vehicle. It could hold twice the medium capacity and was easier to maintain. Of the Mk6s and Mk6As sent to RAF stations abroad, all ended their service life in the UK.

TOTAL NUMBERS

The RAF had eighty-nine, the British Army one, the Royal Ceylon Air Force one and the Royal Canadian Air Force thirty-four, making a total of 125 production vehicles, although according to different sources of information this number may vary slightly, and does not include the prototypes. A far cry from the original forecast of 500. But for all its shortcomings, the Salamander was the first of its kind, an exceptional, if expensive and complex vehicle from which the Defence Fire Services had learned many useful lessons.

Technical Specification, RAF FV651 (Mk6, 6B) and FV652 (Mk6A, C, D)

Engine	
Type	One Rolls-Royce B81 Mk 8A in-line eight-cylinder petrol engine, cast-iron monobloc construction with detachable cast-iron cylinder head. Inlet-over-exhaust valves. Dry-sump lubrication
Bore	3¾in (95.25mm)
Stroke	4½in (114.29mm)
Capacity	6,522cc
Compression ratio	7.25:1
Power	235bhp at 4,000rpm
Torque	314lb ft at 2,700rpm
Governed speed	4,000rpm
Ignition type	Coil 24v
Transmission	
Gearbox	Five-speed pre-selector, fluid coupling
Transfer box	Forward and reverse, giving five forward and five reverse speeds, plus power take-off
Differential	Single, centrally mounted four-star
Propeller shafts	Splined sleeve
Axles	Articulating shafts with two Tracta joints per driveshaft
Hub gearing	4.125:1 double epicyclic
Capacities	
Engine oil	3.5gal (15.9ltr)
Coolant	7gal (32ltr)
Power steering fluid tank	3gal (13.6ltr)
Fuel: Main tank	26gal (118.2ltr)
Fuel: Reserve tank	7gal (32ltr)
Brakes	
Foot	Hydraulic, drums on all wheels
Hand	Mechanical, rod to all wheels
Servo mechanism	Air assisted
Steering	
System	Recirculating ball, divided
Servo mechanism	Hydraulic
Suspension	Independent on all six wheels, with unequal length wishbones and longitudinal torsion bars with sleeves giving 10in total travel. Damping by hydraulic shock absorbers and rebound dampers, two of each per front and rear wheel station, two shock absorbers and one rebound damper per centre wheel station
Wheels and Tyres	
Wheels	Light alloy WD divided disc
Tyre size	14.00 × 20 cross country, incorporated mechanical tyre pump
Dimensions	
Length	19ft 6in (5.95m)
Height	10ft (3m)
Width	8ft 6in (2.6m)
Track	6ft 8½in (2.1m)
Wheelbase	10ft (3m) overall (5ft, 5ft between wheel centres)
Ground clearance	1ft 6in (0.5m)

Turning circle	50ft (15.3m)
Weight, laden	Mk6, 6A, 6B: 12.6 tons (12,813kg) Mk6C, D: 12. 55 tons (12,762kg)
Crew	Six, including driver
Performance	
Max road speed	45mph (72km/h)
Max speed cross country	25mph (40km/h)
Bodywork	Light alloy frame with light alloy panels by Pyrene of Brentford, Middlesex. Totally enclosed cab insulated with mineral wool to render the vehicle operable in a wide range of climatic conditions
Electrical Equipment	24v DC for chassis, lighting and auxiliaries, plus 240v 50 cycle arc equipment for mains-operated equipment used to keep vehicle prepared for immediate action

Firefighting Equipment

The fire fighting equipment fitted to the RAF Mk6 was to MoD specification AD2/SRD/837/P. The main fire-fighting media carried was water and foam. The water was carried in a 700gal (3,180ltr) water tank, the foam compound in a 100gal (455ltr) aluminium tank delivered from either a monitor on the roof or through hoses fitted in the side of the vehicle. It was produced on demand by mixing a foam medium with water and pumped on the FV651 by a Coventry Climax UPF Mk2A centrifugal pump with primer combining with air blower and water pump to produce 9,000gal (40,900ltr) of foam in two minutes. Delivery was by a monitor mounted on the roof. The later FV652 was fitted with a different pump, the Coventry Climax UPF Mk7D without primer, and a fibreglass foam tank in place of the FV651's aluminium one. The roof-mounted foam monitor was designed to operate through a hatch in the cab roof, and had an elevation of 45 degrees and a traverse of 135 degrees. A further medium was also available for use on small oil or petrol fires, pressurized by a cylinder of nitrogen at 125lb/sq.in in a 16-gallon (73ltr) container and delivered by hoses at a pressure of 1800lb/sq.in. On the FV651 this was chlorobromodifluoromethane (CBM) with the hoses wound on reels. On the FV652 this was replaced by bromochlorodifluoromethane (BCF) with hoses layered behind grilles. For cutting into a crashed aircraft, a pneumatic circular saw was provided: sparks from an electric or petrol-powered saw could easily re-ignite a fire. Axes, cable cutters, croppers, handsaws, crowbars and blankets were stored in the cab, as were hand-operated extinguishers. Large crowbars, ladders and grappling hooks were stored on the roof. A searchlight was mounted in the rear of the vehicle.

Technical Specification, RCAF G19 (FV652 Chassis)

As per RAF version with the following differences:

Transmission	
Transfer box	Forward and reverse, giving five forward and five reverse speeds, plus split power take-off to drive foam pumps whilst vehicle is moving
Bodywork	Light alloy frame with light alloy panels by Pyrene of Brentford, Middlesex. Totally enclosed cab insulated with mineral wool to render the vehicle operable in a wide range of climatic conditions. Swingfire petrol-fired pulse heater for cab, capable of producing 30,000 BTUs/hr

Firefighting Equipment

700gal (3,180ltr) aluminium water tank, 100gal (455ltr) aluminium foam compound tank combining with air blower and water pump to produce 9,000gal (40.900ltr) of foam in two minutes, dispensed through hand-operated monitor on cab roof. Ladders and various axes, bill hooks, cutters and other hand tools.

6 The Saladin

Development of the FV601 Saladin continued, albeit slowly, at Alvis alongside the production of the FV603 and the development work of the FV651. The idea of a four-man crew was still argued by the FVRDE until, after consultation with Alvis's gunnery man, Ted Smith, the REME Maintenance Advisory Group recommended the removal of the fourth crew member. The armaments were finally decided and this would settle the discussion about the crew. The main gun would be a new 76mm designed by the Royal Ammunition Research Design Establishment (RARDE) and made by the British Ordnance Factory in Leeds, Yorkshire. Also, the commander's .50 anti-aircraft gun was replaced by a .30 calibre gun and the fire control equipment was redesigned. Interior space in the Saladin was tight and a four-man crew would have fitted at pinch if the 2-pounder gun had been retained but the 76mm gun needed bigger ammunition, and there simply was not enough room for it and a fourth crew member. With three, there would be room for the 76mm rounds and also room for more ammunition for the machine gun. The Army decided that the commander would act as the gunner, the driver would remain at his post and the third crew member would load and man the machine gun, use the radio and act as the rear driver. The recommendation was accepted and a second prototype, FV601B, was built and delivered in 1953. But with a three-man crew the idea of a rear driver was finally abandoned and there would be no rear driving position.

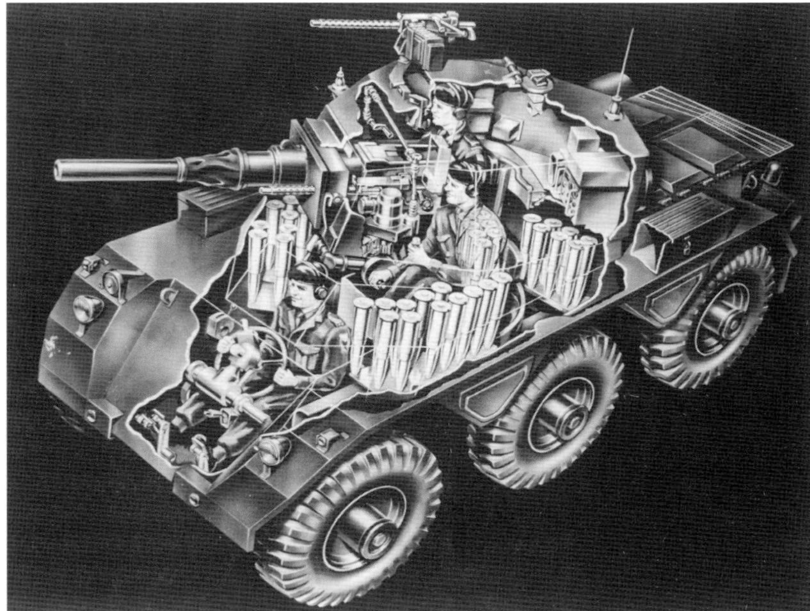

This cutaway picture, used in the Saladin brochure, shows just how tight space was in the vehicle. The commander and gunner needed to work in very close co-operation. (Tank Museum, Bovington)

FV601 Saladin – Vehicle Specification

Engine	
Type – Mk2	One Rolls-Royce B80 No. 1 Mk6D in-line eight-cylinder petrol engine, monobloc cast-iron construction. Inlet-over-exhaust valves. Detachable cast-iron cylinder head. Dry-sump lubrication
Capacity	5,765cc
Bore	3½in (88.9mm)
Stroke	4½in (114.29mm)
Compression ratio	6.4:1
Power	160bhp at 3,750rpm
Torque	257lb ft at 1,750rpm
Governed speed	3,750rpm
Ignition type	Coil, 24v
Transmission	
Gearbox	Five-speed pre-selector, fluid coupling
Transfer box	Forward and reverse, giving five forward and five reverse speeds
Differential	Single, centrally mounted
Propeller shafts	Muff coupling
Axles	Articulating shafts with two Tracta joints per shaft
Hub gearing	4.125:1 double epicyclic
Capacities	
Engine oil	3.5gal (15.9ltr)
Coolant	7.5gal (34ltr)
Gearbox oil	20 pints (11.36ltr)
Fuel tank	53gal (240.9ltr) (including 11gal (50ltr) reserve)
Brakes	
Foot	Hydraulic, power operated 16½in ring type
Hand	Mechanical on all wheels
Servo mechanism	Hydraulic
Steering	
System	Recirculating ball, divided
Servo mechanism	Hydraulic
Suspension	Independent on all six wheels, with unequal length wishbones and longitudinal torsion bars with sleeves giving 10in (254mm) total travel. Damping by hydraulic shock absorbers and rebound dampers, two of each per front and rear wheel station, two shock absorbers and one rebound damper per centre wheel station
Wheels and Tyres	
Wheel type	B8.00-20in, WD divided disc, light alloy
Tyres	12.00 × 20 RF (Run flat)
Dimensions	
Length over gun barrel	17ft 2in (5.2m)
Length, hull only	16ft 0¾in (4.89m)
Height to periscope	7ft 8¾in (2.36m)
Height to turret top	7ft 1½in (2.17m)
Width overall	8ft 4in (2.5m)
Track	6ft 8¼in (2.04m)
Wheelbase	10ft (3.05m) overall (5ft 0in, 5ft 0in between axles)
Ground clearance, unladen	1ft 5⅛in (0.44m)
Turning circle	48ft (14.6m)

FV601 Saladin – Vehicle Specification (*cont.*)	
Weight	
Unladen	20,160lb (9,144kg)
Laden	24,864lb (11,278kg)
Fording Capability	
Unprepared	3ft 6in (1.1m)
Prepared	7ft (2.1m)
Crew	Three – commander, plus driver and gunner
Performance	
Max range (road)	250 miles (400km)
(Cross country)	140 miles (225km)
Max speed (road)	35mph (56km/h)
(Cross country)	20mph (32km/h)
Angle of approach, front	60 degrees
Angle of departure, rear	50 degrees
Ditch crossing	5ft (1.5m)
Electrical Equipment	24v negative earth system, with additional charging facilities for special role and APC vehicles via portable generators mounted on wings
Armament	
Main gun	76mm Armoured C. L5 A1
Machine guns	.50 coaxial in turret, Browning .30 machine gun No. 2, Mk3
Equipment	
Radio installation	No 19, Mk3 and 3/1, or B47 or C12
Sight, periscopic	AFV, No 17, Mk1
	Optical fire control systems
	Smoke dischargers

In October 1955 the Ministry of Supply asked Alvis for one quote for between 150 and 250 vehicles and another for 350 vehicles. The price would be in the region of £100,000. This could, the Ministry suggested, be offset by overseas sales, which might exceed those of the Saracen. Alvis at this time were still fully engaged in the production of the Saracen and had decided to subcontract out the Salamander chassis, and they felt they had no room to make the Saladin. A Manchester firm, Crossley Motors, who had a long pedigree in producing military vehicles, was chosen in 1956 to make the fourteen prototypes of the latest variant, the FV601C. The duties of the crew were also altered. Now the commander should load and the gunner should use the radio.

The first prototype built by Crossley was tested at Errwood Park, Stockport, the site of their bus factory. For some reason, now unknown, Crossley would not allow their testers to take this nor the second vehicle to the Royal Armoured Corps camp at Bovington, Dorset, for testing. But if Crossley had any ambitions on building the Saladin, they were in vain. The MoS had agreed that Alvis would be the official parent of the project, so they would have the first option to make the vehicle. This option they would take: Saracen production would be tailing off but Salamander production was expected to be high. In the event there would be just forty FV651s made for the initial Ministry of Supply order and there would be room after all for Alvis to make the Saladin at Coventry. But the end would come for Crossley in 1958 when Associated Commercial Vehicles, who owned the company, closed the Errwood Park plant. Only six of the fourteen Saladin prototypes scheduled by Crossley were delivered, all receiving government-allocated civilian number plates, as is customary for military

An early Mk2 production Saladin, numbered FV603C, delivered to the War Office but yet to be allocated to a regiment. (Roland Andrews)

The FV601C, nearside view. This was a Royal Armoured Corps vehicle. (Martin Wickham)

vehicles not delivered to the army. The first, RGX 880, was delivered to the MoS in December 1956. This vehicle is now in the Tank Museum, Bovington.

In the spring of 1956 Alvis received a verbal notification of an order for 169 production vehicles, numbered as FV601Cs. This would soon be followed by confirmation in writing. Delivery of the vehicle, also known as the Mk2, was scheduled to commence from November 1957 and be completed by March 1959. After the vehicle maintenance examination on one of the pre-production vehicles, the 76mm gun was fitted on a mount designed by Alvis and gunnery trials were undertaken. But delivery of the gun would hold up production through 1958 due to problems with the embodiment loan. Delivery actually began in mid-1958 but, by the end of the year, Alvis anticipated that thirty vehicles were likely to be held up because of the supply of guns. In May 1958 a further order for 100 Saladins arrived from the Ministry of Supply. Fifteen of these would be for Australia, due for delivery the following year. But the following February the MoS asked Alvis to slow the supply of 601s because of the problems encountered with the delivery of the guns.

W.M. 'Willie' Dunn, who retired from Alvis in 1959. He had joined Alvis in 1922 and at the time of his retirement he had been responsible for the design of the three FV600s that had entered production. But he would be back... (Mike Dunn)

Willie Dunn reached retirement age at the end of 1959 and left the company. He had stayed with the company long enough to see the first of his FV600 projects, the Saladin, enter service. He was replaced by Jack Jones, who came to Alvis from the West Bromwich sports car maker Jensen. In 1959 vehicle delivery began to British Army units in Malaya, Aden, Hong Kong and Germany.

GENERAL DESCRIPTION

The Saladin FV601 is a six-wheel-drive armoured car. It carries a crew of three: a commander/loader, a driver and a gunner/radio operator. It is armed with a 76mm AC L5A1 gun and two .30in Browning machine guns, one coaxially mounted in the turret and a second mounted outside the turret for anti-aircraft and close ground-work by the commander.

The hull is of armour plate and of an all-welded construction, divided into three: a driver's compartment, a fighting compartment and an engine compartment. The whole hull is sealed against the ingress of water. The driver's compartment is at the front of the vehicle. It contains the driver's seat and controls, and is accessed either by a hatch on the front of the hull or from the fighting compartment when the turret is in a suitable position. The driver is provided with three No. 17 periscopes for use when the vehicle is closed down.

The fighting compartment is in the centre of the vehicle. It is fitted with a turret of welded armour plate, mounted on a ballrace on top of the hull. It has a 360-degree traverse. The commander/loader sits on the right-hand side of the turret and the gunner/operator on the left. Hatches are provided

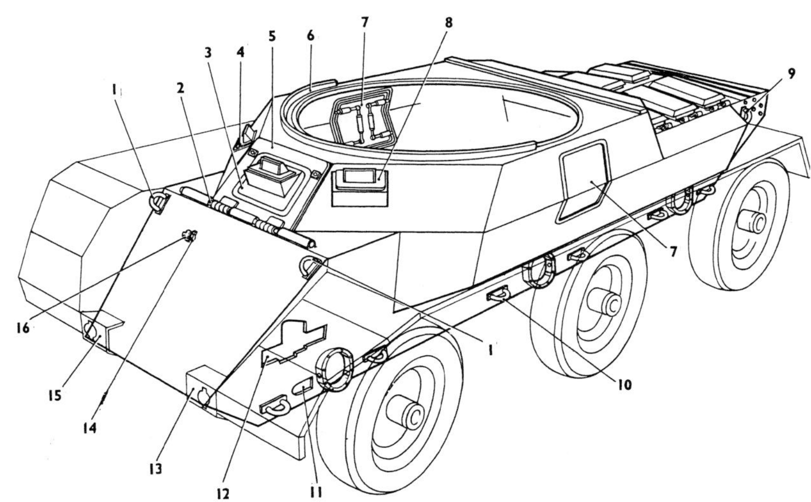

Three-Quarter Front View of Hull.

1 Front lifting eye
2 Torsion bar hinge
3 Visor flap
4 Right-hand periscope housing
5 Driver's hatch
6 Turret ring protection strip
7 Side escape hatch
8 Left-hand periscope housing
9 Rear lifting eye
10 Lashing eye
11 Left-hand steering pocket
12 Aperture for left-hand steering shaft assembly
13 Left-hand driver's step
14 Driver's escape hatch catch
15 Right-hand driver's step
16 Rubber buffer

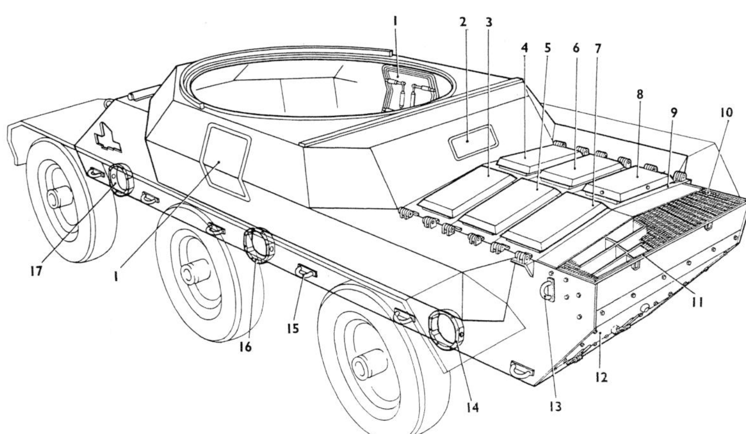

Three-Quarter Rear View of Hull.

1 Side escape hatch
2 Rear observation flap
3 Left-hand front engine cover
4 Right-hand front engine cover
5 Left-hand centre engine cover
6 Right-hand centre engine cover
7 Left-hand rear engine cover
8 Air inlet louvre lid
9 Right-hand rear engine cover
10 Air outlet louvre guard
11 Air outlet louvre assembly
12 Detachable rear skid plate
13 Rear lifting eye
14 Right-hand front and left-hand rear bevel box mounting flange
17 Left-hand front and right-hand rear bevel box mounting flange

in the top of the turret, one each for the commander/loader and gunner/radio operator. Their seats are mounted in the turret turntable, along with stowage space. Apertures in the turntable give access to various components to facilitate servicing. Wireless sets are mounted in the rear of the turret in a special recess. The turret is traversed by a power-assisted manual operation using a torque amplifier and a traverse gearbox unit, and the commander has a separate manual control should the power-assisted system fail. Emergency hatches are fitted on each side of the fighting compart-

The FV601 turret.(Tank Museum, Bovington)

The Rolls-Royce B80 No.1 Mk6D engine from the Saladin. The massive generator, driven by twin vee-belts, can be seen. The other vee-belts drive the power take-off. (Martin Wickham)

ment, jettisonable by means of quick-release catches. Batteries, carbon dioxide cylinders for fighting engine compartment fires, and the drinking water tank are located in the rear of the fighting compartment.

The engine compartment is at the rear of the vehicle. The engine is a Rolls-Royce B80 No.1 Mk6D straight-eight petrol engine, mounted on a four-point mounting. Cooling air enters the engine bay via six louvred, hinged engine compartment access doors and is passed through the rear-mounted radiator by two fans, belt driven off the engine. Air exits the compartment through an aperture on the rear of the top surface. The engine compartment contains three interconnected fuel tanks, one at the left-hand front and one on each side. The oil tank for the dry-sump engine is fitted on the rear of the floor of the engine compartment. A hinged oil cooler is fitted transversely above the engine.

Saladins on the production line during final assembly. The nearside rear bevel box and driveshaft can be seen in the engine compartment. This particular picture also shows a changeover in production from Saracen, at the far end of the line, to Saladin. (Martin Wickham)

Saladins in final assembly have the cast steel suspension wishbones fitted. The side escape hatch can be seen. (Martin Wickham)

The transmission is a five-speed pre-selector type with a fluid flywheel. This is coupled to a single-speed transfer box that incorporates a differential and a forward-and-reverse gear. Drive goes from the transfer box to a driveshaft either side, to bevel boxes adjacent to the centre driving wheels. From the bevel boxes, driveshafts go forward and rearwards to bevel boxes adjacent to the front and rear wheels. From each bevel box a short driveshaft with Tracta joints at each end takes power to

'The Alvis' was always a happy place to work. The haircuts of some of the younger men date this picture, taken with a Saladin that was likely in for reconditioning, to the early 1970s. Test driver Tommy Packham is third from the right. (Roland Andrews)

the wheels. These shafts are coupled to reduction hubs with planetary gears at the wheel end.

The suspension is fully independent, with unequal length wishbones and longitudinal torsion bars. Double-acting shock absorbers and rebound dampers are fitted, two each per wheel, mounted on the lower wishbones at all wheel stations. Servo-assisted hydraulic disc brakes are fitted on all wheels. A mechanical handbrake operates on all wheels. The steering is of the recirculating ball type, hydraulically assisted and operating on the front and centre wheels. The wheels are MoD split-rim type, fitted with run-flat tyres.

OVERSEAS SALES

The Saladin was the most numerous of the FV600 variants, fulfilling the Ministry of Supply's prediction. Of the 1,661 made, 1,418 went to overseas customers. The largest number went to South Africa, who took delivery of 280. This was more than the 243 that the British Army operated. Middle East and other African countries were big buyers. Many were newly independent Commonwealth countries or those enjoying increased oil revenues, all wishing to ensure their security by building up their armed forces. Iraq bought 250, Libya, Kuwait and Lebanon took 100 each, Sudan ninety, Uganda and North Yemen fifty each, Sharjah seventy, Nigeria and Jordan thirty each, Qatar twenty-seven, Tunisia twenty, Ghana nine and Kenya three. Further east, Indonesia, in 1960 the first foreign country to order Saladins, bought sixty-eight, Ceylon (now Sri Lanka) took eighteen and Hong Kong ten.

Apart from Germany, the only other European country to order the Saladin was Portugal, who bought thirty. Switzerland was interested, but after lengthy trials with Saladin pitted against other models, the Swiss came down in favour of tracked vehicles. Malaya expressed an interest. However, they opted for the smaller Ferret armoured car.

Some of the sales were hampered by financial or political constraints. In 1962 Ghana asked for a quote for 25–50 Saladins and 25–100 Saracens, but the Board of Trade export licence was dependent on Export Credit Guarantees and, as we have seen, only nine Saladins went to Ghana, in addition to twenty-six Ferrets. Occasionally, alternative arrangements were made, either due to delivery

Saladins for shipment to West Germany for use by the Bundesgrenzschutz, the Federal Border Police. They would be used for patrol duties along the border between West Germany and Communist East Germany. (Tank Museum, Bovington)

problems or the overall cost of the vehicles; fourteen Saladins that were in service with the British Army were sold on to Kuwait, being replaced with the same number of new vehicles. In 1971 an export licence for thirty-six further Saladins to Uganda was stopped, thanks to the British government's dislike of the oppressive regime of President Idi Amin. Overseas sales of the Saladin would last through most of the 1960s. In September 1965, Alvis's board of directors were told that orders in hand for 629 vehicles would last to August 1967.

GERMAN SALADINS

In January 1964 an order for eighty Saladins for the Bundesgrenzschutz, the West German federal border police, was confirmed. Delivery commenced in October 1965 at a price of £14,625 per unit. These differed only slightly from the standard Saladin in that no coaxial machine gun was fitted, and the commander's armament was a NATO standard 7.62mm gun in place of the .30 Browning.

OTHER PLANS – STALWARTIZED SALADINS

The Saladin's performance with the B80 was said by Alvis's test drivers to be adequate, if a little flat. In May 1965 a 'Stalwartized' Saladin with disc brakes, Stalwart suspension and a 6.5ltr B81 engine was considered for overseas sales. Alvis's representatives met with the War Office to ask them if they could loan a Saladin to them for 'Stalwartizing'. The project would cost an estimated £250,000, in two phases. In phase I, three prototypes would be built and in phase II, six vehicles. This plan was considered to be over-expensive, so Alvis would build just one vehicle. A new turret was proposed for it but not followed through.

In the event, two prototypes would be built in June 1966 at Alvis's expense, but in the event the job took more than six months, with modifications having to be made to the gearbox and the cooling to cope with the more powerful engine. In Alvis's view the new version was worth the effort. One of Alvis's test drivers, Tom Packham, described the hybrid vehicle's performance as 'being like a

One modification tried on Saladin was to fit a 90mm gun. (Tank Museum, Bovington)

Saladins in final assembly. The picture gives a good idea of the huge number of components that went into these vehicles. Behind the Saladins are a number of Saracens on the high level track having the wheel stations fitted. (Martin Wickham)

sports car – it transformed it!' However, the end users were not convinced that an upgrade of an ageing design was the right way to go. One Stalwartized Saladin was completed by October 1966, but the British Army decided that it did not want it. The other prototype, uncompleted, was made available to the US Army, but they chose not to collect it. Production Saladins would keep the B80 as originally specified.

During the Second World War the German used an eight-wheeled armoured car, the SdKfz 234, and the concept was taken up after the war by both West Germany and France. One of the West German vehicles, the Spähpanzer Luchs, was examined by Alvis engineers at one stage with the idea of producing their own eight-wheeler, based on the Saladin but larger. However, the additional complications of the extra two wheels contributed nothing to the capabilities of the six-wheeler. In fact they detracted from it, as it was found to be unstable on hard roads. Thus the idea of a British eight-wheeled vehicle was dropped.

Some Saladins were fitted with diesel engines on an experimental basis and a number of types, including a four-cylinder Detroit two-stroke, were under consideration. The engine chosen for further testing was a six-cylinder Perkins and it performed as well, if not better than, the B80 version. However, the Ministry of Defence, either wanting to retain petrol as a front-line fuel or considering dual-fuel engines, were not convinced that it was a viable vehicle. These projects were hampered by the legacy of Saladin's postponed development. It was already facing obsolescence as its production neared its end. Had not the Malayan crisis put Saladin on hold, it may have been more plentiful in the British Army and perhaps seen much further development. As it was, the next generation, the CVR(T) series of tracked reconnaissance vehicles from Alvis and the FV430 tracked vehicles from GKN were already around. Saladin's potential would remain untapped.

NOTE ON VEHICLE IDENTIFICATION

Unlike the other FV600s there was just one production model Saladin, the FV603C, otherwise known as the Mk2 (the Mk1 being a prototype). As such there is no need to provide a section on vehicle identification.

7 'The Floating Packing Case' – The Development of the Stalwart

The annexation of eastern European countries by the Soviet Union after the end of the Second World War triggered the four-decade standoff that was the Cold War. In 1949 the allies in the west formed NATO, the North Atlantic Treaty Organization. Created by Russia to oppose to them from the other side of the Iron Curtain was the Warsaw Pact, which included its satellite states of Poland, Czechoslovakia, the Baltic States, Hungary, Rumania and, most significantly for this chapter, the German Democratic Republic – East Germany. The belief in the west was that if a third world war were to be started by the Soviets, there would first be an 'exchange' of atomic weapons to destroy each others' cities, followed by a massive land battle fought across Europe.

This would be a fast-moving war like the Nazis' Blitzkreig, but on a much greater scale. Tanks would be in the forefront of the battle and these would have to be supplied by equally fast support vehicles. Much of Germany is criss-crossed by rivers and it was naturally assumed that Soviet forces would destroy the bridges that spanned them. For sappers to erect enough extra bridges in time to allow the Allies passage would be a logistical impossibility, so support vehicles would have to have an amphibious capability. None of the wheeled trucks in service were anywhere near fast enough, nor had sufficient off-road performance to keep up with the tanks, nor possessed the required amphibious capability. The nearest was the wartime American DUKW, a ship-to-shore vehicle that, because of its long bow structure, would be handicapped by steep riverbanks. Besides, the few that were still in service were in reserve stock. Added to this equation was the decision to abolish conscription, the tool by which Britain was able to police its former colonies, which were by now gaining independence. Britain's army would be reduced to 180,000 men by 1960. The emphasis was to be on a highly trained, highly mobile force with top quality equipment.

The Defence Review of 1957, that had such an effect on the fate of the Salamander, would by chance give Alvis the opportunity to recoup something of what they would not achieve in terms of sales with that project. And in the process Alvis would design and build one of the British Army's most unique and distinctive vehicles. The Secretary of State for War said in 1957 in his memorandum of Army Estates: 'We plan to produce a family of weapons with no supplementary or overlapping members. This family will provide an armoury which is a fine balance between the needs of limited operations on the one hand and global war on the other.'

The FV600 had already shown what the Secretary of State meant in principle, but he was not referring to those vehicles, rather to their replacement, GKN Sankey's FV432, that was being evaluated by the British Army at the time. The War Office was investigating the requirement for a load carrier with amphibious capability and had plans to see if a version of the FV432 would fit the bill. Willie Dunn heard of this and approached the War Office to ask them to consider a load-carrier version of the FV600. His arguments were that the chassis had well proven cross-country performance and fording capability. Wheeled vehicles in comparison to tracked vehicles were known to be quieter in operation, were easier to service with longer service intervals and were cheaper to make. They were easier to drive and this, coupled with the lower noise level, resulted in a lower level of crew fatigue. Also, wheels cause far less damage to roads and lines of communication than do tracks, and the lower rolling resistance of wheels meant that fuel consumption was less. All these factors were borne out by the experience gained by the Army using the Saracen.

The War Office, or to be more specific the Military Vehicle Engineering Establishment (MVEE) at Chertsey, were unconvinced: they were already committed to the FV432. However, Alvis had a man on their side who would be a great asset and, indeed, could be given the credit for first putting forward the idea of Stalwart. He was Alvis's sales manager, Major W.D.P. Sullivan. 'Sully', as he was known, had retired from the Royal Armoured Corps where he had been the officer in charge of the official equipment trials. But he still retained contacts within the War Office and, of course, he knew his way around 'the system'. He had discovered that the RAC were concerned with supplying front-line troops with ammunition in battle, especially in Northern Europe, as part of Britain's commitment to the NATO force. Sullivan knew from his own experience that the trucks supplying the tanks and armoured cars needed not only fast cross-country ability, but an amphibious capability too.

PV1

Sullivan had been carrying out his own research, gathering not just positive feedback but actual serious enquiries. In mid-May 1957, Alvis's board gave the go-ahead for the building of a prototype High Mobility Load Carrier on a Slamander hull. Under Willie Dunn's direction, Alan Russell in the design office laid out plans for a prototype vehicle to see if the concept would work. It was given the tag PV1, as this was a private venture on the part of Alvis, and it was completed by December 16 1959. It was evident that the chassis and running gear could carry considerable weight: the Saladin and Saracen were 10 and 11 tons respectively and a fully laden Salamander weighed 12½tons. The

PV1 photographed at the rear of Alvis's factory. Its Salamander parentage is very clear. The drop sides are an entirely conventional design. (Martin Wickham)

'The Beastie', undergoing trials. A Citroën 2CV pick-up, used by the Royal Marines as a light air-portable truck, is lowered onto a flatbed trailer from a Westland Whirlwind helicopter. The cargo deck of PV1 has been converted to a flatbed. A much smaller Skeeter helicopter could be carried on it. (Martin Wickham)

basic chassis was fitted with a shortened Salamander cab, with standard side doors and deeper windows. As a load carrier the vehicle would require a basic dropside body. The sides, for testing purposes, were easy enough to fabricate, although arriving at a successful waterproof design that was both light and strong would take some considerable work. It was not possible to build a flat floor on the Salamander chassis. The engine cover and the air intake for the mid-mounted radiator stood higher than the deck, necessitating the division of the load area in two. With its oversized tyres and boxy cab, it lacked the elegant proportions of the Saladin or the purposeful stance of either the Saracen or the Salamander. It was nothing short of ugly and it soon earned the nickname 'the Beastie'.

A load, consisting of a huge number of Jerry cans filled with water, was placed onto the cargo area to test the load-carrying capability. Immediately it was realized that this split deck would be of no use and that subsequent test vehicles would have to have a flat bed. However, the vehicle would serve the purpose of providing enough information for Alvis to take the project further.

The new vehicle was announced in 1960 and, in the first three months of that year, Alvis undertook a considerable amount of testing on public highways, especially the A45 Coventry by-pass (this fast road was a favourite 'test track' for the city's motor manufacturers) and at MIRA, the Motor Industry Research Establishment. Off-road trials were carried out at Cannock Chase and wading trials at Kingsbury Water, Tamworth. These proved that the chassis was adequate for the job, although it must be said that this was almost a foregone conclusion, considering the excellent duty that Saracen had given over the previous decade!

A NEW NAME

During the early days of PV1's progress, Willie Dunn went out for the day with his family. On the trip was his son, Mike, at home from university. Willie Dunn mentioned that he was working on a new vehicle and that it needed a name. It had to begin with 'S' and when Mike heard of its role he suggested, out of the blue, 'Stalwart'. His father liked it and the HMLC now had a name.

INTO THE WATER

Saracen, and Saladin for that matter, could swim, given the right equipment. Here at Instow some flexible ducting has been added to allow the radiator and engine to function whilst it swam, with the water almost to the top of the hull. (Roland Andrews)

Both the Saladin and Saracen had undergone flotation trials at the REME Fording Trials establishment Instow, the Saracen fitted with elaborate snorkels and the Saladin with a flotation screen. It had proved the hulls to be watertight, but although PV1's hull was built in the same way as its predecessors, its superstructure was entirely different. The cab had full-height doors and the load bed had no sealing around the drop sides, so PV1's load deck and the cab doors needed to be waterproofed in some way. For the purposes of the trials, drop sides were fitted to the deck and waterproof sheets were wrapped around the sides and cab. PV1 was taken to the flooded quarry at Stoney Cove in Leicestershire. Water-filled jerrycans weighing a total of 5 tons were loaded on the vehicle. Divers were present, as the water at Stoney Cove was, and still is, very deep. One can imagine the trepidation of the driver and attending crew as PV1 was driven cautiously into the water. It floated, but there was very little freeboard. Further tests were made at old Gravel pits at Coleshill in Birmingham, which were chosen for safety's sake, as they were nowhere near as deep as Stoney Cove.

When the War Office were approached with the project, they were, to say the least, upset that Alvis had 'gone round the back door' and had already got so far with an idea that was still, to them, secret and not even put out to tender. However, they had acceded to the Army's wishes, and in April 1960 issued a GSOR stating a requirement for a 5 ton wheeled load carrier. The specification included these requirements:

- To carry a payload of 5 tons
- To have a cross-country performance superior to that of the Saladin and Saracen but equal to that of most tracked vehicles of comparable size and load
- To have a maximum road speed of about 50mph (80km/h) to allow rapid transit and delivery
- Low internal and external noise factors essential for operational purposes
- Improved crew comfort and a reduction in driver fatigue
- Improved access to engine and transmission
- To minimize maintenance and user training due to the similarity in mechanical layout to that of the existing FV600 vehicles already in service.

Now the project had gained official recognition and in April 1960, immediately after the specification was received, PV1 was taken to the FVRDE at Chertsey. From then until November it underwent trials both at Chertsey and at the Royal Armoured Corps at Bovington, Dorset. PV1 was to be pitted against the FV432 prototype tracked carrier to see if a wheeled vehicle was in any or all respects better for the job. In the event, FV432's manufacturer was unable to present a vehicle for testing. Whatever reservations Chertsey had about PV1, and these would be certainly coloured by the fact that it was a private venture and a different concept from their own, the Army were very pleased. The trials now were cut to a load-carrying assessment, at Bagshot Heath, Surrey, Salisbury Plain and Lulworth Heath.

Amphibious trials of PV1 took place at Instow. The vehicle was carefully taken into the sea, again with divers on board to ensure that the driver was rescued in good time if the vehicle should sink. The Army described PV1's performance as 'favourable'.

THE FERGUSON CONNECTION

At this time, Alvis had taken out an agreement with FFD, the Coventry firm founded by Tony Rolt and Freddie Dixon with tractor pioneer Harry Ferguson, to make a passenger car with all-wheel drive and anti-skid brakes. FFD were developing a centre differential, which would obviate transmission wind-up in a vehicle with permanent four-wheel drive. Alvis was developing for use a 1 ton all-wheel-drive army truck and had taken out an agreement to use FFD patents. FFD technology was considered for use on the new HMLC vehicle as a cure for the endemic wind-up problem, particularly as its role might involve a fair degree of convoy work on hard roads. However, the FFD system would not be included, the existing driveline would be carried over and also the new project was given priority over the one-tonner.

PV2

'The Beastie' proved that the concept of an amphibious wheeled load-carrier based around the FV600 hull was a viable one. Whilst Alvis's engineers knew that a simply modified Salamander was, as it stood, nowhere near suitable, it gave them an excellent starting point. There were four main areas of design that needed attention: the hull design, the powertrain, the cab and the cargo deck. What had not been considered was a full amphibious capability. British Army A and B vehicles, that is to say fully armoured and combat zone vehicles, had to have the ability to wade ashore, but the FVRDE extended the requirement of the HMLC to one of full amphibious capability. After all, the FV430 series were fully amphibious. Now there was not only a requirement to make the hull and superstructure watertight, but to provide a suitable form of drive in water. A new prototype, PV2, would be built to develop the vehicle further. Sanction for this was given by the board in May 1960 and authorization to build given at the end of the following December, whilst PV1 was undergoing its initial trials.

With the knowledge gained from PV1, Fred Phillips set out a basic design for PV2. When PV1 was floated, it had a very low freeboard. This meant that conventional side cab doors were out of the question, however watertight they were made. Access for the crew would have to be through the roof and a square, sliding hatch was included in the design. The centre driving position of PV1 was retained. A one-eighth-scale model was built and taken to the test tanks at Saunders Roe's premises in the Isle of Wight to find out if it would work, to see what sort of speed it was capable of, and to discover just how the full-size vehicle would behave. The most noticeable shortcoming was poor visibility in water, as the bow wave rose up above the windscreen at any sort of speed. To overcome this, the whole of the hull was re-profiled, with a far less blunt front end. The rear was extended too, and the new vehicle was 20ft 6in (6.25m) long, some 18in (0.5m) longer than the Salamander. A washboard was built into the design to divert the bow wave to either side. This consisted of a plywood board hinged in half that folded flat against the front of the vehicle when not in use.

The engine would be a Rolls-Royce B81, as it was in the Salamander, but PV2's would be a Mk8B, de-tuned to produce a net 213bhp at the slightly lower speed of 3,750rpm and would be able to run on standard Army fuel. The vehicle was to be a prime mover, not a combat vehicle. The preselector gearbox was considered, but not chosen. So was a fully automatic gearbox, but if all the wheels on one side of the vehicle leave the ground, the gearbox's changing mechanism detects the resulting rise in revolutions and becomes confused. Instead a five-speed Meadows synchromesh gearbox was used, as it would enable the engine to

Technical Specification – Mk1 (FV620)

Engine	
Type	One Rolls-Royce B81 Mk8B in-line eight-cylinder petrol engine, cast-iron monobloc construction. Inlet-over-exhaust valves. Detachable iron cylinder head. Dry-sump lubrication
Bore	3¾in (95.2mm)
Stroke	4½in (114.3mm)
Capacity	6,516cc
Power	220bhp at 4,000rpm
Torque (nett)	312lb ft at 2,400rpm
Compression ratio	6.4:1
Governed speed	3,750rpm
Ignition type	Coil 24v
Transmission	
Gearbox	Five-speed Meadows manual, synchromesh on second, third, fourth and top gears
Clutch	Borg and Beck twin 12in dry plate
Transfer box	Single range, forward and reverse, giving five forward and five reverse speeds, plus power take-off
Differential	Single, centrally mounted, 'No Spin' device
Propeller shafts	Splined sleeve
Axles	Articulating shafts with two Tracta joints per shaft
Hub gearing	4.125:1 double epicyclic
Overall ratios	First 103:1, Second 53.83:1, Third 33.24:1, Fourth 19.83:1, Top 12.9:1
Power take-off	Marine propulsion unit and winch hydraulic pump
Drive in water	Two Dowty 12in diameter units driven from PTO on gearbox
Capacities	
Engine oil	3.5gal (15.9ltr)
Coolant	7gal (32ltr)
Gearbox oil	2.5gal (11.4ltr)
Fuel tank	100gal (455ltr)
Brakes	
Foot	Lockheed calliper-operated discs on all wheels
Hand	Mechanical, via transmission-band type on front bevel box drums
Servo mechanism	Air servo
Steering	
System	Recirculating ball on front and centre axles, power assisted
Servo mechanism	Hydraulic
Suspension	Independent on all six wheels, with unequal length wishbones and longitudinal torsion bars with sleeves giving 10in total travel. Damping by hydraulic shock absorbers and rebound dampers, two of each per front and rear wheel station, two shock absorbers and one rebound damper per centre wheel station
Wheels and Tyres	
Wheels	Divided disc, 10.00 × 20
Tyre size	14.00 × 20 ten-ply
Dimensions	
Length	20ft 6⅞in (6.27m)
Height unladen	8ft 3½in (2.54m)

Technical Specification – Mk1 (FV620) (*cont.*)

Width	8ft 4in (2.54m)
Track	6ft 8 5/16in (2.04m)
Wheelbase	10ft (3m) overall (5ft, 5ft)
Ground clearance, unladen	1ft 4 1/2in (0.42m)
Turning circle	45ft (13.7m)
Weight, unladen	18,592lb (8,400kg)
Laden (land use)	29,792lb (13,500kg)
Fording Capability	To full flotation
Crew Capacity	Driver, plus one crew member in cab.
Performance	
Max road speed	43mph (67km/h)
Max speed cross-country	20mph (32km/h)
Max speed in water	5 knots
Max gradient	24 degrees
Max vertical obstacle	1ft 6in (0.46m)
Max approach angle	44 degrees
Max departure angle	35 degrees
Max trench crossing	5ft (1.5m)
Max gradient	18 degrees (1 in 3)
Side unladen overturn	37 degrees
Range	450 miles (640–720km)
Load capacity	5 tons (5,080kg)
Electrical Equipment	24v DC negative earth for chassis, lighting and auxiliaries
Miscellaneous Equipment	Six towing eyes, one at each corner of the vehicle, each capable of taking the full towing load and two situated on side plates at the front of the vehicle. One towing hook fitted at the centre of the rear skid plate
Maritime Equipment	Detachable rope or rubber fenders at each corner, navigation lighting to international maritime law
Special Equipment	Fire extinguishing equipment around engine and fuel tank

be used for braking. An American design No-Spin differential was chosen for similar reasons, despite the fact that they tended to be more stressful on the gears. The well-proven transfer box and driveline from the other FV600 vehicles was included, although the final drive ratios were reduced. This would reduce the maximum speed to about 45mph (72km/h) and cope with the fact that the vehicle would be carrying 5 tons across country and be encountering some steep gradients.

The steering would be power-assisted, as in the previous vehicles, but the steering wheel would not be totally central. Willie Dunn had retired from the company and his replacement, Jack Jones, insisted that as it was a British vehicle it had to be right-hand drive. The others on the design team told Jones that it was not possible to do this to any great extent. In any case it was a pointless exercise; the army were not bothered and it would save the job of having to make a left-hand drive export model. Still, Jones had his way after a fashion, as the steering was adapted so that the wheel was all of 2 1/2 in (70mm) to the right of centre.

The brakes would be completely different. Brake technology had moved on considerably from where it was around 1947 when development of the FV600 series had begun, and calliper-operated disc brakes were by this time optional equipment on a small number of private cars, including Jaguar. As the Stalwart was to swim across a river

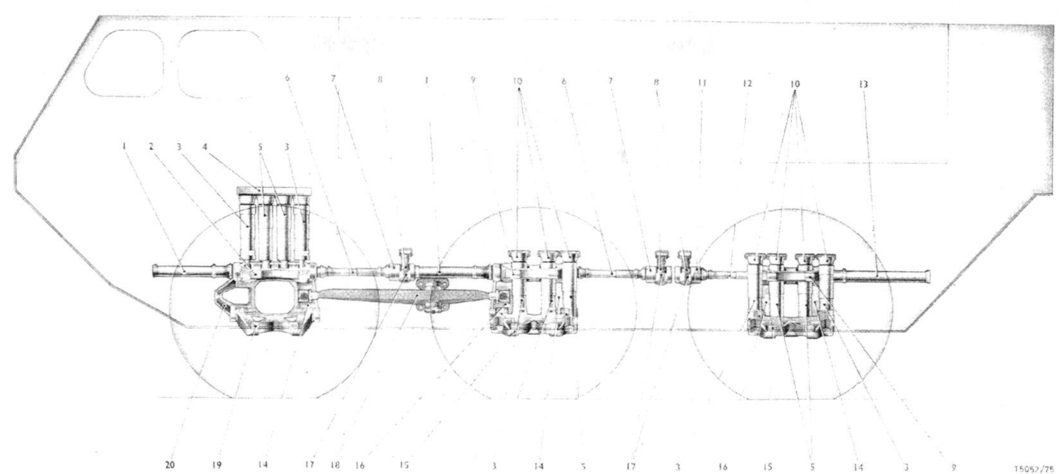

Suspension Layout.

1 Sleeve – front end and centre torsion bars
2 Top link – front
3 Bump and rebound dampers
4 Mounting block – damper and shock absorber
5 Shock absorbers
6 Torsion bars
7 Bracket – adjusting lever
8 Adjusting nut – torsion bar
9 Top link – centre and rear
10 Anchor housings – damper and shock absorber
11 Bracket – adjusting lever
12 Torsion bar – rear
13 Sleeve – rear torsion bar
14 Link bracket – rear
15 Bottom link – centre and rear
16 Link bracket – centre
17 Adjusting lever
18 Steering lever (rocking beam)
19 Bottom link – front
20 Link bracket – front

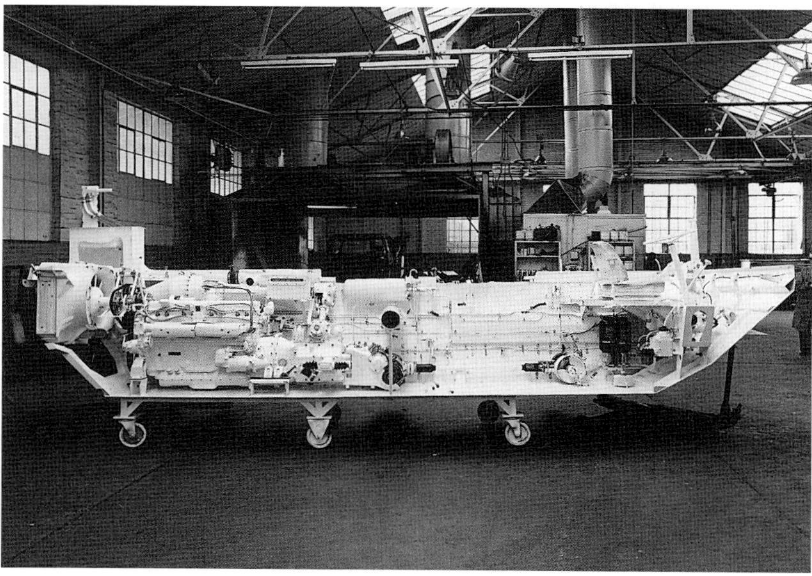

A Stalwart hull cut in two for demonstration and training purposes. Seen clearly, from left to right, are: the radiator and fans, the engine, above which is a propulsion unit, the clutch housing, the gearbox and the transfer box with its power take-off and driveshaft to the propulsion units. Central is a large tubular cross member, below which is the differential with drive to the centre wheel stations. Running forward is the drive-shaft to the front wheel station, inboard of which is the contracting type handbrake. To the front are the (virtually!) central steering wheel and the long gear lever. (Martin Wickham)

and immediately be driven on land, the need for brakes that would dry out very quickly was imperative. So was the need for brakes that would stop a vehicle weighing in excess of 13 tons over hilly country. The drums as used on the Saracen and Salamander would not be of any use when leaving water and the Saladin's ring brakes were, in design terms, a blind alley. Alvis approached AP Lockheed with a view to producing modern disc brakes for Stalwart. Lockheed were at the time working on disc brakes for the twin-steer Bedford VAL coach, the drum brakes of which were notoriously poor. Although some concerns were expressed as to whether there would be enough disc-pad area, the job presented no real difficulties and it amounted to a scaling up of those used on such cars as the Wolseley 6/99. A solid disc system with air-assisted triple-circuit operation, one circuit for each axle, was developed and tested at the same time as the rest of the vehicle. Disc systems did not at the time lend themselves readily to a handbrake function – even the disc handbrake on Jaguar's automatic models relied on a separate hydraulic backup – and so a separate contracting-band-type handbrake was installed inboard of the discs on the front wheels.

PV1's drive in water was the same as it was for Saladin and Saracen, simply by means of the wheels paddling it along. For PV2 two Saro-Gill two-stage jet propulsion units were fitted inside the hull either side of the engine, powered from a PTO fitted to the gearbox. These would give a speed in water of 4.5 knots and provide a steering facility, controlled by a horizontally mounted tiller in the cab.

The engine and radiator covers of PV1 were done away with and a totally flat load deck designed. This deck was also at the same level as the Chieftain main battle tank, making the transfer of ammunition in the field a simpler task. The Salamander air intake was removed and a ducting system fabricated to take air in from the rear of the cab roof, the highest point of the vehicle. The air outlet from the radiator was in the form of a grille in the rear of the cargo deck, but this of course could not be left unprotected. A removable bulkhead was built forward of it, the full height of the drop sides, which prevented any cargo from covering the outlet. This created an enclosed box, with a drop tailgate to allow access to it.

There were three criteria that governed the design of the drop sides. One was that they should be rigid enough to be watertight, second that they should be light enough to be lowered and raised by two men of average strength, and three, be strong and light enough to hold the load should it shift. The first design was double skinned, incorporating six indented panels on the outer skin, running the full length of the cargo bed. The tailboard was constructed in the same manner. A compressible rubber seal around the lower edge and uprights provided waterproofing.

BRITISH ARMY TRIALS WITH PV2

PV2 was sent for trials with the army at Bicester, Warminster, Hankley Common, Bagshot Heath and Long Valley in the early part of 1961. Now it was tested against the FV431. The War Office was still unhappy at the idea of Alvis 'getting in via the back door', especially with a vehicle that did not meet their original concept, but Alvis's argument was that they would have their vehicle two years earlier than if they had gone with the FV432. But the Army favoured PV2. Swimming trials took place in April 1961, at Instow. Here turbulent currents are created as the River Taw meets the Bristol Channel and the Atlantic Ocean. As waves of 10ft (3m) or more were encountered, much was learned about how the Stalwart would cope in rough seas and how to drive it in surf.

In June 1961 the War Office, perhaps still smarting as a result of Alvis's effrontery, considered that the Stalwart was a DUKW replacement and thus its requirements would be no more than 100 vehicles. It urged Alvis to reconsider the project. John Parkes did not agree with this and decided to talk to Gloster-Saro and Vosper, who were the experts in marine propulsion. By August 1961 the

PV2 during its swimming trials at Instow. The drop sides are full length, made up of strengthened rectangular panels. Just visible behind it is the DUKW used as a tender vehicle and at the water's edge is a BARV, a Beach Armoured Recovery Vehicle based on the wartime Sherman tank. (Martin Wickham)

War Office had seemed to change its mind, and stated its intention to order nine Stalwarts for trials. A third prototype was sanctioned as a result of this. They further discussed the specification with a view to a pre-production contract and, as a result of a conference between the War Office, the Treasury and the Fighting Vehicle Directorate, the War Office informed Alvis that they would place an order for the nine prototypes.

SWEDEN

An encouraging development occurred very early in Stalwart's lifetime when the Swedish Navy showed interest. Although Sweden was, and still is a neutral country, it nevertheless is security minded. Its southeastern coastline faces the former Soviet Baltic States. Further east is the Gulf of Finland, at the head of which is the Russian city known in Soviet times as Leningrad. Thus the security of the southeast coast of Sweden depended on a chain of six offshore batteries, armed with 75mm guns, missiles and mine-laying facilities. Keeping these supplied were a fleet of boats. In action the loading and unloading of ammunition from trucks to boats took a considerable time and the Swedish Navy, who manned the batteries, took a keen interest in the Stalwart. They envisaged a fleet of these vehicles being able to carry supplies directly to the batteries without the need to load and unload onto boats.

PV2 was sent to Sweden in September 1961 where it was exhibited at the St Erik's Fair in Stockholm and also shown to the NATO Study Board. It then went to the Swedish Naval Coastal Artillery for trials. Two modifications were made to the vehicle before it went to Sweden. The big square roof hatch was too heavy and cumbersome and was replaced by a smaller circular hatch that hinged sideways, fitted in the plate that covered the hole left by the original hatch. Secondly, as PV2 was likely to encounter some steep slopes in Sweden when exiting the water, an upright freeboard

PV2 in Sweden, about to descend the rocky shoreline into the water. The extension above the rear of the load bed is just visible. (Martin Wickham)

extension was added to the rear to prevent water from getting into the engine compartment and the load deck.

Accompanied by Major Sullivan and other Alvis representatives, the Swedish Navy put PV2 through its paces. They were particularly interested in the vehicle's ability to enter and leave the water off the steep rocky slopes of the shoreline, far harder ground than the farmland of central Europe for which the Stalwart was intended. It was driven out of the water over the severely sloped rock shores, where the extension at the rear of the vehicle was found to be adequate, and through dense woodland. At one point in its swimming trials a gunboat was driven past, creating a bow wave, with the intent to test PV2's stability.

In September 1961, following these trials, PV2 was taken back to Alvis in Coventry, from whence it would eventually commence trials with the British Army. A Swedish technical mission planned a visit to the Alvis works. Clearly the Swedish Navy were satisfied as they ordered two more vehicles, which would be numbered PV4 and PV5.

PV3

The third prototype, PV3, was already under construction whilst PV2 was undergoing trials and it would include some modifications already brought to light by the results of the work done by PV2. Putting them in PV3 whilst it was under construction would save time as well as giving all concerned a further vehicle for evaluation.

A trailer hitch and air brake lines were fitted, as well as two circular roof hatches. Another highly significant modification proposed by the Army, but never carried out on their behalf, was the installation of a multi-fuel engine. The powerplant was to be a Rolls-Royce K60, but the amount of work needed to install it, modifying the cooling system and completely rearranging the driveline, as well as the increased weight, meant that the idea was shelved. However, a fully automatic gearbox, made by General Motors Corporation's Allison Division was fitted in PV3 and the combination of the K60 multi-fuel engine and the Allison gearbox was considered by Alvis's board as a possibility in

Alvis got extremely good value out of PV2. Here it is undergoing trials with the Army, fitted with the second type of drop side and the new section for the radiator air outlet. (MBRT, Coventry)

a significantly modified Mk2 Stalwart.

In November 1961, PV3 went to the army for trials. Normally these would have been spread over a distance of 10–15,000 miles (16,000–24,000 km) over the cross-country course, through simulated alpine work and fresh and salt-water amphibious trials. However, thanks to the work undertaken with PV2 these were shortened to 5,000 miles (8,000km). Undertaken at FVRDE Chertsey and Long Valley, Aldershot, with the alpine tests carried out at Bagshot Heath, they were split into fourteen stages, seven laden and seven unladen. PV3 did not perform as well as its predecessors. Some eighty-five separate component failures were found. The Allison gearbox was troublesome, draining power from the engine, and despite the hope that it would reduce crew fatigue, in practice it had a slow, difficult shifting mechanism and lowered the top speed on the vehicle by 9mph (14.5km/h). The cooling system was inadequate, as was the exhaust, and the brakes were not performing up to expectations.

Swimming trials took place at the end of 1961 at Horsea Island, Portchester, Hampshire, with PV2. The Saro-Gill propulsion units were found to be inadequate for the job. And with a payload of 5tons the freeboard was too low for safety in anything but calm water, risking flooding of the vehicle.

PV4, PV5

Modifications were made to PV4 and PV5 during the course of their construction, both to fit their new role and to correct faults discovered with PV3. The fan and radiator size was increased and the air intakes re-routed. PV2's exhaust came out behind the cab and this caused problems. Its side-hinged circular hatch was replaced by two forward-hinged hexagonal ones. The Saro-Gill cascade drive was not up to the job. It could not provide enough thrust to maintain a decent speed in water and it was too vulnerable to damage by debris. George Dowty took a great interest in the Stalwart project and offered to develop a water turbine. Given working drawings, his company designed the new drive units, but they were not sure of how to provide steering in a hull that was different from the boats in which Dowty turbine drives were installed. Back at Alvis's head office, Fred Phillips designed what he termed 'buckets' to direct the drive, as well as

The two Dowty propulsion units, shown at the top left and right of the picture. The drives for them come from the power take-off located on the top of the transfer box. The big rectangular boxes between the propulsion units are the air cleaners. (REME Museum)

The bucket for the left-hand propulsion unit, which enabled the Stalwart to be steered in water. Above the wheel is the inlet. In trials these could get covered in debris and weed. Alvis tried fitting cowls over them but this made the problem worse. In practice the Army had little trouble with debris, opting to carry a bass broom to clean them off after a swim. (Bill Munro)

The two large levers in the centre of the picture are the vehicle's rudder controls, operating on the propulsion units. (Bill Munro)

designing controls in the cab. The first trials of the new drive system were at a lake at George Dowty's own mansion close to Gloucester, such was his own interest in the project. The Army undertook further swimming trials with the Dowty propulsion units in PV2 at Horsea in December 1962.

The load was prone to shifting and causing damage to the side panels, so the whole of the load area of PV4 and 5 was redesigned and included retaining lugs. Two designs were considered, one of fibreglass outer skins sandwiching a foam filling. These were very tough, resisting the dropping of a conical weight that represented the corner of a crate. This type was, however, too heavy. The type chosen was constructed of a cellular aluminium core, sandwiched between thin fibreglass panels, with a surround of aluminium channel. The air outlet for the radiator was effectively encased in a box with the exhaust routed alongside it. There would no longer be a drop tailgate. The new panels were also fitted to PV2.

THE SWEDISH NAVY DECIDES

The Swedish Navy had decided that it wanted Stalwart and returned to Alvis with a list of modifications it required. These, to comply with both their own needs and with maritime law, included:

- Navigation lights front and rear
- Trailer service points fitted to the rear of the cargo area and behind the divided bulkhead
- External lashing points incorporated in the side panels for use alongside jetties and for the attachment of fenders
- A wooden rubbing strip included on the top of the side panels for protection against harbour and jetty walls
- Folding bench seats fitted along the inside of the side panels.

Swedish-made 1 1/2 ton Foco cranes were installed on the forward end of the load decks of PV4 and PV5 to enable the loads to be moved quickly and conveniently. Whilst the crane undoubtedly did its job well, its extra weight made the vehicle swim with a nose-down attitude. This impaired forward visibility, so a Plexiglass panel was fitted into the swim boards.

The order by the Swedish Navy for PV4 and PV5 was placed in March 1962 and they were delivered in June at a price of £14,000 each. These vehicles were put through some rigorous testing in the winter conditions and some serious problems arose with the driveshafts and with the sealing of the drop sides. Below a certain temperature the rubber seals would compress but not return to their original shape. Several alternative materials were tried and eventually a neoprene seal was found to be the best.

The Swedish authorities were obviously happy with the vehicle and with Alvis's willingness to solve any and all problems that arose. Although indicating a possible further order of 100 vehicles, by the end of 1962 the Swedish Navy ordered six Stalwarts from Alvis. They would include mountings for the Foco crane, which would be fitted in Sweden.

There would be one further 'problem' that Alvis would surmount with some degree of aplomb. The six vehicles were ready for dispatch and Swedish government inspectors arrived to accept the vehicles formally, but said that they would only take them if they did a 1,000-mile (1,600km) test. A small team of Alvis's test drivers were contacted and asked what they were doing that weekend. Then they were told what they were wanted for – testing six Stalwarts! The team would spend all weekend driving the vehicles built for Sweden from Coventry to London. As each service period came up the vehicles were serviced, the water level in the radiator checked and they were sent straight out again. On Monday morning the six vehicles were lined up and had all done 1,000 miles. The Swedes were, in Fred Phillips' words, 'Absolutely taken aback. They'd never seen anything like it!'

A NEW CHIEF ENGINEER

Jack Jones and Alvis had parted company and Willie Dunn was persuaded to come out of retirement to resume his old job in a temporary capacity. He still retained his loyalty to Alvis after forty years of service, but he would rather be enjoying his retirement and Alvis would need to replace him soon. His replacement would be his own son, Mike, who had been an apprentice at Alvis in the 1950s. After university he joined Ford and was in line for a job with that company in its German operations. However, he had enquired about a job

PV4 and PV5 underwent some severe winter trials in Sweden. Here is one of them being tested in snow. It was in these trials that the rubber seals of the drop sides were found to be susceptible to extremely low temperatures. Note the drop sides, of a sandwiched construction, and the separate section to the rear of the load bed to accommodate the air outlet from the radiator. (Mike Dunn)

with Alvis as a development engineer. Alvis went one better and offered him the job of chief engineer, starting in October 1962.

WELDING AND PAINTING

Willie Dunn had found what would seem to be the ideal steel with which to make Stalwart's hull. It was Cor-ten, a low-alloy steel made by the Steel Company of Wales. This would have enabled a thinner gauge to be used and thus reduce the weight of the vehicle to 8½ tons. However, the Steel Company of Wales's owners, the British Steel Corporation, were cutting back on production and, as the demand for Cor-ten was very low, ceased its production. Only a handful of prototypes were made of Cor-ten and the material chosen for the main production run was BS968 steel. This material presented its own challenges in the fabrication of the hull. The new process of CO_2 fine-wire welding was selected, as the wire was low in hydrogen content and prevented the discoloration of the paint by the flux residues left by manual metal arc welding. A further advantage of CO_2 welding was that the joints in the hull could be of a different design, one that did not require welding on both sides. This would speed up the manufacturing process and, as a result, lower costs. As Stalwart was to be swum in seawater, a full epoxy corrosion-proof paint, with a zinc-rich primer was used.

Mk1s on the production line, in final assembly. The cabs were made by another Coventry firm, Motor Panels Ltd. The twin radiator fans can be seen in the vehicle in the foreground. (Martin Wickham)

Already Alvis were investigating the commercial possibilities of Stalwart. In September 1962, PV2 was exhibited at the Commercial Motor Show at Earls Court. Painted yellow, it was not amphibious, having side doors instead of roof hatches. Although it must have created a great deal of curiosity, there was no serious interest shown.

DRIVESHAFT PROBLEMS

The FVRDE's deputy director H.C. Bradfield told Mike Dunn that he did not like the Stalwart, and it was not simply because Alvis had supplanted the FV432. His dislike was for a specific technical reason, namely the unreliability of the Tracta joints. Mike Dunn decided to prove FVRDE wrong. There were failures with the Tracta joints on the Swedish vehicles due to apparent lack of lubrication. At the time all Alvis could do was strip them down, replace them and hope they would not fail again. An attempt to alter the faces of the joints to facilitate better lubrication did not succeed.

The answer came to light when it was found that driveshafts in vehicles that had been swimming were contaminated with water. It appeared that the hub oil-seal was letting in water, but it was Alvis's

The instrument panels and controls of the Mk1 Stalwart. The cylindrical tank between the instrument panels is the brake fluid reservoir. The batteries are behind the partition to the right of the picture. (Bill Munro)

The Mk1's swim board in the partially unfolded position. The operation necessitated one of the crew to dismount to carry it out. (Bill Munro)

engineer Jack Hedges who found the problem. A breather valve in the hub was set to blow off at a pressure of 1.5psi, and draw air in at 0.5psi. The breather valve was replaced with a union and a pipe fitted above the height of the chassis to allow it just to suck in air, with a sight glass. As the pressure rose and fell with the speed of the vehicle, so the level of oil in the sight glass rose and fell. The change in the temperature of the oil was causing it to be blown out. The problem was aggravated as the Army were overfilling the driveshafts. When taken swimming the seawater rapidly cooled the driveshafts, reducing the pressure and drawing in seawater. Now the problem had been identified the valve could be changed and the Tracta joint problems disappeared.

THE ARMY ACCEPTS STALWART

By the end of summer 1962, Alvis's work seemed to be paying off when 125 Stalwarts were ordered for the British Army. They were to be delivered over twelve months and would be designated FV620. The batch would include the next prototype in line, PV6, and seven more, PV7–13. The problems with the side panels had been solved. After experiments with the two other designs had proven to be unsuitable, a design that consisted of two sheets of aluminium, a corrugated outer and a flat inner, was designed. This gave the necessary resistance to bowing out, and provided a good seal.

The first forty-four vehicles were delivered to the Army in July 1963. In November, six vehicles

23 EK 96 (STAL 61) was made around the middle of the Mk1 production run. Here it is acting as a limber vehicle for a Centurion tank. The swim board is seen in its fully folded position. The final corrugated design of drop side is clear, with vertical and horizontal strakes added for strength. The horizontal strake actually saved a life. A soldier very nearly fell under the wheels of a Stalwart, only preventing himself from doing so by grabbing hold of the strake. (Martin Wickham)

were sent to Bovington for six months of acceptance trials. The remainder went to the Royal Corps of Transport at Borden, Hampshire, then to Germany in service alongside tank regiments as load carriers. A small number of Stalwarts were sent to Aden for weather trials where they worked well with 1st Armoured Division Transport Regiment in Radfan. They were returned in August 1964.

Swimming trials were held at Instow, Gareloch, Strathclyde and Poole Harbour. The low freeboard when loaded with a full 5 tons was not liked by the Army when driven offshore and thus they limited it to 3 tons when swimming.

PV10 was included in the first batch of Stalwarts delivered to the Army. It was given the Army registration mark 23 EK 50 and would remain at Instow with the REME Fording Trials Unit. It would serve in the same safety and back-up role as the old DUKW had when PV1 and PV2 were first swum there and, as such, became known as the 'divers vehicle'. PV6 would not enter service with the British Army but be sold to Italy in 1964.

GEARBOX DIFFICULTIES

During the acceptance trials trouble was experienced with the Meadows synchromesh gearbox. Meadows modified it by using a Porsche design of split-ring synchromesh. The improved boxes were scheduled to be delivered by March, but when installed they continued to give trouble. Mike Dunn brought in gearbox expert Ivor Giles. His job was to beef up the gearbox by metal spraying part of the synchromesh apparatus to provide a hard-wearing surface. In December 1964 the manufacturing rights to the Meadows gearbox were transferred to Alvis.

BAOR TESTS

In February of 1964 Major Sullivan reported to the board that he was pleased with how Stalwart was performing in the RASC trials with the BAOR, but all was not as well as it appeared. There had to be an official acceptance of the vehicle by the Army and the meeting that would grant it had been postponed until 17 June after BAOR tests were completed. However, the RAC trials at Bovington were thought 'likely to be favourable' despite the troubles experienced with the gearbox. In October 1964, to help things along, Alvis sent two Alvis fitter/instructors to the REME at BAOR. The official acceptance meeting was not until March 1965, when Alvis were invited to formally present Stalwart.

The FVRDE were generally happy with the Stalwart despite niggling little troubles so often found in early examples of any motor vehicle. They found that the vehicle's cooling was much improved over the prototypes' and to confirm what was already understood, said that its external noise level was much lower than the FV432. In November 1964, 325 Stalwarts were ordered for the British Army, with delivery to commence from February 1966 at a maximum of twenty-four per month. But the Army were already looking at what improvements could be made.

8 The Mk2 Stalwart

Almost like a sea monster rising from the deep, a Mk2 joins a Mk1. (Martin Wickham)

It was clear from the very start that the British Army, or at least the staff charged with testing it, wanted the Stalwart. Even the later tests against the FV431 HMLC failed to shift the Army from its choice. There were hold ups, however, in the awarding of the formal contract due to disagreement over the final production specification and, when the contract was sent to Alvis in May 1965, it was returned for amendments. The final version did not arrive until July 1965. After six years of work, the HMLC project had gone from the seeds of PV1 to fruition in the form of FV620.

There were detail improvements to the FV620 that the Army wanted to see, but these would not be built into the existing vehicle. They would be included in an upgraded model, a Mk2 Stalwart. The specification for the Mk2 was with Alvis in April 1965 even before the contract for the Mk1 was finalized, let alone signed. These arose as a result of the 1964 trials of FV620, which from now on would be called the Mk1.

The modifications were quite straightforward. There would be no 'super Stalwart', to coin a phrase, with a multi-fuel engine and a fully automatic gearbox. So far as the Army was concerned, Alvis had got 'Stolly' more or less right. The required changes were:

- Improved driver visibility
- Improved cab layout
- Increased braking efficiency
- Self-recovery winch
- Driver maintenance to be reduced
- Redesigned swim board
- Air portability.

Development of the Mk2 began when STAL 56, the fortieth production vehicle, was taken from the tracks at Alvis and modified. The improvements to the brakes were Lockheed's job and they fitted a second brake master cylinder and an Air pac tank, but everything else was rectified without too much difficulty at Alvis.

Apart from the method of fixing, Stalwart's cab windows were unchanged from those fitted to PV2. This was one of the reasons for the poor visibility, aggravated by the central driving position. Perhaps Jack Jones had had a point when he wanted right-hand drive! The other was the height of the vehicle. But the solution was quite simple for Motor Panels, the makers of the cab, to carry out and it was also connected to the second of the Army's requirements, an improved cab layout. The Mk1 had a partition to the driver's right, behind which were the batteries. This precluded the installation of a third seat in the cab. To improve the visibility, the outer windscreen and the front side-glasses were reshaped so that the lower edges were sloped down. If the partition had remained, it would have obscured the driver's vision out of the larger glass area. This was especially important when operating in Germany, as a good view of the kerb, on the driver's right, was essential for safety. The whole of the cab area was redesigned, with a new instrument panel and a third seat to the right of the driver.

A winch was required for self-recovery. A hydraulically operated one made by Boughton was chosen, to be powered by a pump driven from a modified power take-off. It would be installed behind the bow plate, in a watertight compartment. But with the winch located so close behind the bow plate, the cable would meet the drum at an acute angle, which compromised its ability to spool neatly. After much discussion between Alan Russell and Mike Dunn, a swinging carrier was designed that presented the cable to the drum at a constant right angle, ensuring the cable spooled evenly across the drum.

*The Mk2's cab with the redesigned instrument panel. The absence of the partition (*see *page 127) makes for a clear line of sight out of the enlarged windows. (Bill Munro)*

An early Mk2 Stalwart photographed at Alvis's factory. The most obvious difference between it and the Mk1 is the shape of the cab windows. The alteration to the top front corner of the front bulkhead to enable it to be loaded into a transport plane is detectable. There is the line of the join above the fire extinguisher. Also new is the spotlight on the roof, the front towing attachment and the revised swim board mechanism. The winch cable runs from the front of the bow plate, up the offside corner of the cab to a fixing point on the rear of the roof. Note the small driving mirrors – later ones were bigger. (Martin Wickham)

PV7 is tried out for its fit into an RCAF Hercules. (Martin Wickham)

The troubles encountered with the Tracta joints very early on presented a solution to the question of reduced vehicle maintenance. There were a lot of lubrication points on the Mk1. The tubes that Jack Hedges had connected to the troublesome breather valves suggested something that Alvis had used on some of its pre-war cars – central chassis lubrication. There was a large tubular cross-member in the hull and this was used as an oil reservoir for the driveshafts, eliminating the long job of having to top up each individually. Mike Dunn envisaged connecting the front and rear bevel boxes (the centre ones were lubricated by the differential oil) to the system, but this was not carried out.

Erecting the swim board on the Mk1 was a lengthy process. A crew member had to dismount, undo a couple of wing nuts, fold down the board and locate a couple of metal stay rods. In battle this was not just impractical; it could be life threatening. A mechanism was designed whereby the swim board could be unfolded by two crew members leaning out of the top hatches over the front of the vehicle.

Air portability was a growing requirement as Britain's forces had shrunk in size. Now rapid deployment was the byword and that meant big planes that could carry vehicles. The RAF had two, the Blackburn Beverley and the new Armstrong Whitworth Argosy. Soon to come into service was the even bigger Short Belfast. This plane was a good design, but it would only be established with 53 Squadron, which would be reformed at RAF Fairford in 1966 specifically to operate it. Soon to be adopted by the RAF was the Lockheed Hercules, which had only just come into service with the US Air Force. In 1965 the RAF had yet to receive the Hercules and the PV7 was tried for size in an example borrowed from the Royal Canadian Air Force. It was found that the top front corners of the load bed were fouling the opening in the aircraft. The Mk2s were therefore modified so that these corners could be unbolted to allow the vehicle to be loaded onto the plane.

The Dowty propulsion units were retained, and further additions included a roof-mounted spotlight, rear mud flaps, a front towing attachment and, last but not least, a cooking vessel for that vital brew-up.

Designated FV622, the Mk2 Stalwart was accepted into service by the British Army in early 1966 and delivery would commence from 1967. The British Army would take most of Stalwart production, in both Mk1 and Mk2 form.

STALWART IN AMERICA

PV8 (registered by the British Army as 24 EK 71) was destined to travel far. Aberdeen Proving Grounds in Maryland, USA had seen all of the American Army's vehicles, good and bad, including such famous ones as the Sherman tank and the

Alvis had their own test tank at the rear of the factory. This early Mk2 has been anchored down to test the propulsion units. Incidentally, a dunking in the test tank was a part of the 'passing out' ceremony for Alvis apprentices! (Martin Wickham)

A Mk1 Stalwart on display at the 1964 Farnborough Air Show. It carries a Swingfire wire-guided missile system and the cab is mocked up to give the impression of armour plating. The Army considered arming PV1 and adding armour plating. The additional weight ruled this plan out. Saladin was tested with Swingfire, but it was the tracked FV438 that would be the British Army's principal carrier. (MBRT, Coventry)

jeep. It was a requirement of NATO that each constituent country should make its military equipment available to the others. From July to September 1963, with a short spell at the Transportation Board at Fort Story, Virginia, for water trials, PV8 went to Aberdeen, Maryland, for evaluation. Although there were a lot of detail problems and a major one when the engine threw a connecting rod, the response to Stalwart was generally favourable. In fact, the Mack truck manufacturing concern expressed an interest in a co-operative manufacturing deal if the US Army were to take their interest further and consider ordering it.

The Stalwart's handling in water was described as 'very good', its ride and suspension 'excellent' and it was credited as being comparatively quiet. But this was just an analysis. No sales were expected, nor orders received.

A single bright red Mk2, equipped with a monitor, was sold to Thailand for use as a fire crash rescue vehicle at Bangkok Airport. (Martin Wickham)

FV623 LIMBER VEHICLE

It may have been noticed that there was a gap in Stalwart model numbers. If the Mk1 Stalwart was FV620, and the Mk2 was FV622, where was FV621? The short answer is that the truth is lost to the memory of most concerned with it, but a reasonable guess was that it was first earmarked for a Mk1 artillery limber vehicle.

In 1961 the War Office issued GSOR 1088 stating a requirement for such a vehicle to support tanks and self-propelled artillery. The idea that Stalwart could fit this bill had been with Alvis since then. It was even proposed, as early as 1963, that PV2 should swim across the English Channel, deliver a load to a British Army tank unit in Germany and then fly in an RAF Argosy transport plane from Luneburg to the Paris Air Show. However wonderful a piece of PR this would be it was, of course, never carried out. PV2 was wanted elsewhere.

GSOR 1088 required:

- Compatibility with the self-propelled guns it was to support
- A need to carry ammunition and stores not carried by the gun
- As large a payload as is consistent with other requirements and the tactical environment in which it is to be used – 5 tons being the desirable payload.
- Ammunition must be unloaded and loaded quickly and with minimum effort
- It is desirable that the vehicle should provide the same crew protection as the Abbot self-propelled gun when on the move
- It must accept alternative low-density loads including POL (petrol, oil and lubricants) and rations
- It must be able to supply ammunition to more than one gun.

Stalwart could meet almost all of the above. The only point in this specification where it was found wanting was that of armour plating. Constructing a cab out of armour plate was considered and, considering its simple shape, it would not have been a difficult job to do. But with a full load, Stalwart was already at its weight limit and the weight of the armour, plus the crane would have been excessive.

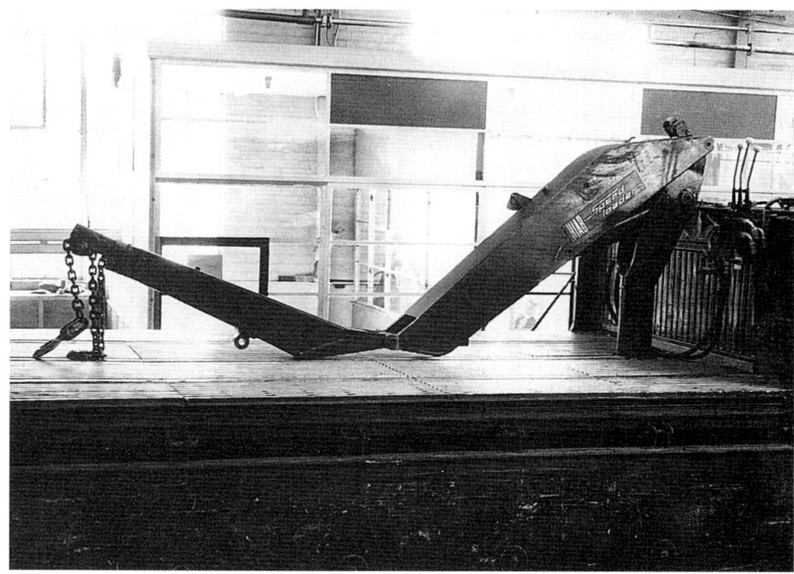

The HIAB crane installed on PV2 prior to the limber-vehicle trials at Larkhill. The levers on the control panel can be seen at the extreme right of the picture. (Mike Dunn)

At Larkhill gunnery school on Salisbury Plain, between January and June 1964, old faithful PV2 would undergo trials as a limber vehicle. Part of the Stalwart's role as a load carrier was the delivery of ammunition, but to speed up the delivery this prototype purpose-built limber vehicle would be fitted with a HIAB hydraulic crane which was already fitted to some Army vehicles. This would be powered by the PTO-driven hydraulic pump that also drove the winch. It was operated by a workstation on the back of the cab roof, the operator standing on a cab seat and halfway out of a roof hatch. Some time during the trials a roller floor was fitted; although it worked well, its cost outweighed its advantages and it was never adopted. That summer, PV2 went home to Coventry where Alvis used the crane in tests to evaluate the Stalwart as transport for a Royal Navy Hiller helicopter.

Whilst the trials had provided some useful data, no final decision had been made over the adoption of Stalwart as a limber vehicle. This was because the Army had begun experimenting with palletized ammunition, and this would protract the matter for at least another two years. In July 1966 the Army had taken a look at another crane, the Atlas Type 3001, which had a capacity of 3 tons. This was much more than the HIAB and they decided it was the one they wanted for palletized ammo. So Alvis were asked to fit the Atlas on PV2 and in January 1967 it was returned to Larkhill. The Army were happy with what they found as a result of the palletized ammunition trials.

The trail of the missing number, FV621, seems to end here. By now delivery of the Mk1, the FV620, had been completed. The new Mk2 Stalwart, FV622, would be the base of the limber vehicle and this would be numbered FV623. If the limber vehicle had been built on a Mk1 it may well have been numbered FV621.

FV623 entered service in late 1967 with the Royal Artillery and would be part of the existing contract for 400 Mk2s already received by Alvis. FV623 carried a crew of seven, including the driver, and, as the cab could only accommodate three, seating for four was provided on the load deck, two

An FV623 fitted with an Atlas 3001 crane lifts a pallet of ammunition. (Reme Museum)

An International half-track of Second World War vintage, used by REME until the 1960s as a recovery vehicle. (REME Museum)

An FV624 REME Fitters vehicle. Compare this with the International half-track above, especially the stowage of the Atlas crane on the Stalwart, as opposed to the unwieldy gantry on the half-track. (REME Museum)

either side, by the crane. A canvas shelter was supplied for the men who had to sit in the back. FV623's role was to support the Vickers-built Abbot 105mm self-propelled gun and the bigger American M107 and M109. Some 269 examples would serve, with twenty-seven in each regiment, excepting those working with the M107, who would receive twelve each.

FV624 REME FITTERS' VEHICLE

The Corps of Royal Electrical and Mechanical Engineers were and are responsible for maintaining all of the British Army's motor vehicles. In the field they had been depending on the American M14 International half-track, a vehicle delivered to the British under Lend-Lease during the Second World War. Although having a reputation as being indestructible, they were well past their prime and a replacement was needed. REME were already aware of the Stalwart limber vehicle trials and felt that a version of this would serve their purpose well.

A REME version of the FV432, the FV434, was under development. This was fully armoured and, of course, a tracked vehicle with all the advantages and disadvantages of its ilk. Whilst the Stalwart could not provide the armour protection that the FV432 could, this disadvantage was nullified for most duties by the Stalwart's 5-ton capacity – the FV434 could only carry 3½ tons. A REME Stalwart could work alongside the FV434. With its armour, the FV434 could work under fire at the 'sharp end', where the Stalwart would be too vulnerable.

Thus, to fulfil this role, the FV624 REME Fitters' Vehicle was evolved out of the FV623. Indeed, the design work of this vehicle was well under way by this time as Alvis were invited to present a prototype vehicle at an Army Acceptance Meeting for Stalwart in March 1965.

The FV624 would have a crane, and it would be the Atlas. But there was a difference between the crane on the FV624 and that on the FV623. REME fitters would be required at times to change an engine in the field on anything from a Land Rover to a Conqueror tank. To do this, the crane's hydraulic mechanism was adapted so that the jib could 'creep' in order to enable the minute adjustments need to manoeuvre an engine, especially in the case of the Chieftain tank, where the L60 engine formed part of a removable power pack, in and out of a tight space.

The REME vehicle would carry a crew of just four: two men including the driver in the cab and two in the rear. Sixty FV624 Stalwarts would enter service and in the field the crews would make them their home, with camp beds and cooking equipment loaded in the rear.

The Berliet Connection

The French firm of Berliet had a long history of truck and car making. They were supplying the French Army with 6×6 4- and 8-tonne trucks and recovery vehicles. These were powered by five- and six-cylinder multi-fuel engines, of which type Berliet were pioneers. Bearing in mind the FVRDE's move towards multi fuel with the K60, Alvis and Berliet got together to discuss a joint venture, whereby Alvis would manufacture a 4×4 Berliet truck with a five-cylinder multi-fuel engine at Coventry for sale in the UK. Berliet would make the Stalwart, which they would call the Aurochs, in France with the intent to sell it to the French Army.

In February 1964, PV15 was sent to Berliet and one Berliet truck was delivered to Alvis. Staffed by very good technical people, especially their sales manager, M. Allegret, Berliet were enthusiastic about the project. So were Alvis. The British Army liked the Berliet truck and there was even interest from London Transport. Berliet believed there was a market for the Stalwart in French Army, and a production Stalwart, STAL 34 went to France to follow PV15. Whilst there was very good co-operation between the two companies, the sales potential did not materialize. The Ministry of Defence were not interested in the Berliet truck nor were the French Army interested in the Aurochs. There would be no commercial advantage so, in 1967, Alvis and Berliet parted company.

Comparing the FV624 with the FV434, one can say that they were 'horses for courses'. Outside of the battle zone where armour was superfluous, the Stalwart was lighter (unladen, by some 5,000kg!), it carried a bigger payload and its wheeled configuration and forward lorry-type cab made it simpler and less tiring to drive. (This could be its disadvantage, as there are stories around of how some squaddies used Stalwarts as runabouts on hard roads, damaging the driveline as a result!) Its tyres would not, of course, damage roads as a tracked vehicle might. We must remember that, although this was the time of the Cold War, an actual state of war did not exist and the BAOR was stationed in a friendly country. There was, it must be said, some resentment by the German population, who had to live alongside the presence of heavy trucks and armour, and large numbers of foreign troops. Thus any damage that the Army incurred to civilian property had to be avoided if feasible, to maintain as much goodwill as possible. In any case the cost of making good any damage came out of the Army budget and this was taxpayers' money.

SPECIAL APPLICATIONS

The Royal Army Medical Corps tested the Stalwart as a field ambulance, but the load height made this impracticable. Trials as a troop carrier proved equally unsuccessful. If seats were fitted permanently they would have to be removed to gain access to the engine. Ranger Barrier Mine equipment was installed on a number of Stalwarts but the installation did not last long and it was the old adversary, the FV432, which would have this job.

OVERSEAS CUSTOMERS

As early as March 1962, the Bundeswehr (the German Army) had shown an interest in Stalwart but, with memories of the Second World War still prevalent, the sale of Stalwarts to Germany was not favoured by War Office. Three years later, in early 1965, the mood had not changed and a request to loan a Stalwart to the German Ministry of Defence was declined. A suggestion by the Defence Supply Attaché in Bonn that the last vehicle of the current batch of Mk1s should be built to the new FV622 specification for use as a demo vehicle was not accepted. However, pressure to deal with Germany prevailed and, following a request to Alvis later in 1965, PV14 was sent to Germany for evaluation. It was registered as Y-04222 and two new Mk2 vehicles followed it. They performed well in the tests the German Army put them through. This was not entirely surprising as the Stalwart was designed to operate in Central Europe. But one odd test was to launch a Stalwart off a pier at speed. Why this was done the Germans did not say. The front of the vehicle was submerged and there was a fear that water would enter the air intakes, flooding the hull. But the vehicle survived and, thankfully, the driver had the sense to shut the roof hatches!

The Germans also wanted to perform an emergency stop on the handbrake alone. This alarmed Alvis's engineers as this contracting-band brake operated solely on the front wheels. To ask it to stop a weight of over 8 tons was asking far too much and Mike Dunn told the English civilian test driver, 'Don't practice!' The test was duly carried out and the vehicle did indeed stop, but the driver heard a distinct bang underneath him. The Germans were deterred from asking for a repeat performance and the crippled Stolly was quickly removed before the wrecked brakes were discovered. The German Army at first ordered 100 vehicles but, in the event, none was delivered as the Bundeswehr opted for the American replacement for the DUKW, the LARC.

PV6 had been demonstrated on the Austrian–Italian border, as it was felt that it would be a useful vehicle to have if the melting winter snows flooded the region. PV6 was sold to Italy and the Austrian Army bought three Mk2s for their internal use.

Six Mk1s had been sold to Sweden and a further order for eighteen Mk2s followed. These would serve until the early 1980s. Some of these vehicles were purchased privately and returned to the UK.

MARINER

The DUKW of the Second World War was a remarkable vehicle, not just for the fact that it was such a simple concept – a boat hull fitted to a GMC truck chassis – but that it worked extremely well. So well, in fact, that some are still in use almost sixty years after they were built. Its function was different from that of the Stalwart. The DUKW was, in effect, a combination of landing craft and load carrier, whereas the Stalwart was a load carrier with amphibious capability. However, it was felt that the DUKWs in service in the British Army by the early 1960s should be replaced. The Stalwart seemed an obvious choice, but there were shortcomings. The Stalwart was designed to swim across rivers and its front end was a compromise between that and the fact that it would spend far more time on land than in water. On the other hand the DUKW bow was shaped to cope with inshore tides. Could the Stalwart be modified to cope with rough seas?

The initial interest came from America, who claimed to want amphibious-cum-cross-country vehicles for service in the Far East. This would mean Vietnam, where the conflict there was beginning to escalate beyond the training and observation duties that the US forces were sent out to perform. One stated requirement was that the vehicle should be capable of being driven through the surf of the Pacific Ocean. Alvis were suspicious: they felt that all the Americans wanted was knowledge, not vehicles. However, they first went to Saro-Gill on the Isle of Wight who, in their huge indoor tank, made surf so that a Stalwart model could be tested. The conclusion of these experiments was that another 3in (75mm) of freeboard was needed and that the vehicle should be lengthened.

Front and rear extension 'tanks' were designed and these were mocked up out of a frame of thin tubes covered with sheet metal. The front tank would be shaped like the bow of a boat, the rear tank like the stern. PV3 was fitted with the extensions and tried out at Stoney Cove. They worked, giving about 6in (150mm) of extra freeboard. Sheet metal tanks would be expensive to make, so the tanks were made out of fibreglass with rubber anti-skid material on the tops to allow personnel to stand on them in safety. But whilst the extensions

PV3 fitted with the 'Mariner' bow and stern extensions, entering the water at Stoney Cove. The ubiquitous water-filled jerrycans are once more put to use. (Martin Wickham)

Operation Mudlark *was aptly named. Here one of the two Stalwarts involved in the trials is rendered immobile by Thailand's muddy tracks. (Alvis Owner Club)*

would be necessary for operating the vehicle in the sea, they would be a handicap when driving on roads and also on entering rivers, which have steep banks not found at the sea shore. Some way, therefore, had to be found to remove the extensions. The American observers were concerned about how the tanks would be jettisoned. It was not a facility that, at this stage, had been resolved, but a solution was soon at hand. Back in the drawing office, Fred Philips designed an explosive bolt that would blow out and drop the tanks once the vehicle had driven up the beach. The operation, including backing up the vehicle to clear the jettisoned tanks, would take three minutes. Trials of the operation, which was quite successful, took place at Stoney Cove. The Americans weren't very impressed but, having gained what they wanted, retired.

MORE TESTS AT INSTOW

In early 1968 the Amphibious Experimental Establishment (AXE) at Instow outlined the principles of design of amphibious vehicles, mainly in the area of safety. AXE made the point that Stalwart was not a true amphibian, not having good seaworthy performance, but its ability to cross a fast-flowing river was found to be lacking and any vehicle operated in such conditions needed to be as safe as a ship-to-shore amphibian. AXE found that the Stalwart's two bilge pumps were inadequate and that the control of its rudders was uncomfortable. They felt that the mechanical steering in water could be replaced by a hydraulic or wire-controlled systems and that its water speed was inadequate. They also expressed a need for a rapid tyre-deflation system to enable soft going to be tackled more effectively. The report went on to suggest that, if the establishment would have access to Alvis engineers, they could work together to produce a much bigger Mk3 vehicle with full sea-going capabilities. Needless to say, this was not followed through.

OPERATION *MUDLARK*

The Far Eastern Land Forces (FARELF) operated often in jungle conditions and in very soft going, and their HQ wanted to know if the Stalwart would cope with their field of operations as a recovery vehicle. The Americans, now deeply involved in the Vietnam War, were keen to discover more. In 1966, Stalwart was pitted against two British and two American tracked recovery vehicles in a programme called, with dubious humour, Operation *Mudlark*. The British vehicles were FV432 (again) and the FV437 Pathfinder, which was an experimental version, designed to recover vehicles from riverbeds. The American vehicles were FMC's M113A1 and a variant of the aluminium M551 Sheridan tank.

Two Stalwarts were dispatched from Singapore and Johore Bahru to the test area in Thailand, both countries being in the same peninsular as Vietnam. The Stalwart, the only wheeled vehicle, fared extremely badly, proving to be mechanically unreliable and not at all suited to soft mud. It was the M551 that was the most successful, which no doubt pleased the Americans.

THE GAN REEF RESCUE VEHICLES

The archipelago of Addu Atoll is a part of the Maldive Islands in the Indian Ocean. During the Second World War the Royal Navy built bases at each end of the archipelago and RAF Catalinas and Sunderlands flew from there. In 1957 a runway was built on the small island of Gan at the extreme south of the archipelago, for the Far Eastern Air Force, RAF, to man as a staging post for British servicemen and families travelling back and forth between the UK and Singapore and Hong Kong.

The station's runway was as long as the island itself and if an aircraft undershot or overshot it would land in the ocean. Thus a special amphibious rescue vehicle was required. An ex-army Stalwart, 00 ER 63, was transferred to the RAF's Far East Air Force at the beginning of 1967 and was renumbered as 00 AG 79. Painted bright yellow, it was used as a fire crash tender, as it could swim out to an aircraft that had landed in the ocean. The hose pickup, with water-resistant bronze fittings, was simply thrown over the side to pump water to fight fires. A dinghy was fitted and rope ladders could be slung over the side to enable survivors to climb aboard. A second Stalwart, 07 ER 57, was transferred to Gan in December 1971 and renumbered 09 AH 16. This vehicle retained its Army olive-drab colour but carried a yellow stripe along its side. Now in the event of one vehicle being unserviceable there was a backup. The Maldives gained independence in 1965, but the RAF continued to

The equipment carried in the Gan Reef Rescue vehicles. This is the first of the two, 00 AG 79. (Alan Godfree)

The second of the Gan Reef Rescue vehicles, 09 AH 16. The pipe coming forward from the load bed is hung into the ocean to draw up water. (Alan Godfree)

operate on Gan until 1976 when both Stalwarts were withdrawn from service.

HOVERCRAFT

The concept of an amphibious vehicle was taken further after the invention and commercial application of the hovercraft. A hovercraft ferry service to the Isle of Wight had recently begun, and cross-channel services were begun in the 1960s. In 1967 the MoD sent an enquiry to the British Hovercraft Corporation to produce a 5-ton load-carrying hovercraft. Alvis were contacted and a model, based on a design using Stalwart hull and running gear built into a hovercraft inflation skirt, constructed. The road engine was to have been a Rover 2S-150 gas turbine and the airscrew was to have been powered by a Rolls-Royce Gnome. Unfortunately, all the hovercraft equipment took up so much room that there was little space for a load and the project was dropped after a year.

DIESEL ENGINES

Some potential overseas customers were asking Alvis about diesel engines and the board agreed that a suitable diesel motor should be found. Berliet made two dual-fuel engines that were in use in military vehicles in the French Army, the larger being a 145bhp six-cylinder. It would not have been powerful enough and did not run at higher than 2,000rpm, which would have necessitated re-gearing the Stalwart. The real problem of finding a suitable diesel was one of the physical size of the engine. As diesel engines of the time produced much less horsepower for a given capacity than a petrol engine, a much larger diesel engine would have to be found. The K60 dual-fuel engine was some 500lb (225kg) heavier than the B81 and the B81 was a big piece of metal in itself. Length would not necessarily be a problem, as the B81 was a straight-eight, but width would, as any wider powerplant would interfere with the water propulsion units. The American company Cummins made V8 diesels that would have been short enough, but too wide; Perkins made six-cylinder engines of adequate power which were high revving. But the biggest customer for Stalwart was the British Army who still were using petrol engines. Overseas sales were nowhere near those achieved by Saracen or Saladin and there was not sufficient commercial viability to warrant the extra costs involved in fitting a diesel engine.

Model Identification

Stalwarts are identified by a mark number and an FVRDE number. Both numbers are used by the British Army, whilst Alvis would simply refer to the mark number. Neither the FV623 nor the FV624 have a separate mark number.

All Stalwarts were powered by the same Rolls-Royce B81 Mk8B engine. The FV622 had a hydraulic pump driven by the power take-off attached to the differential that drove the winch, whilst on the FV623 and FV624 the hydraulic pump also drove the crane. Otherwise all Stalwarts shared the same drivetrain.

Mk1 FV620
The original Stalwart production model, easily identified by its cab windows, which have a horizontal lower edge. The cab has two seats: one in the centre for the driver and a second to his left. The swim board is held down by two thin steel rods, although a lot of Mk1s will have had later-type swim boards fitted.

Mk2 FV622
Recognizable by its enlarged cab windows, giving it a 'droopy eyed' look. The cab has three seats abreast. The swim board has a sliding mechanism and there is a winch and a front towing hook fitted.

FV623
Identical to the FV622 with the exception of a crane and four seats in the load bed.

FV624
Identical to the FV623 but with just two seats in the load bed.

UBRE

An army's performance is only as good as its chain of supply, be it ammunition, food, fuel or whatever. The standard means of supplying fuel to front-line troops since the end of the Second World War was the 5gal jerrycan. This required a lot of hard labour and time, unloading the cans and emptying them into the fuel tanks of the recipient vehicles. And fuel dumps, like arms dumps, are prime targets to an enemy.

In the early 1960s, two new methods of shipping fuel were investigated: a pipeline, favoured by the USA and USSR alike, and a bulk delivery system. The pipeline required a lot of manpower to defend, something that the British Army, after its cutbacks, would not find favourable. The better alternative was bulk refuelling, which was discussed in April 1965. It would operate in the following stages. A bulk store would be established well behind the lines and 22,500ltr (4,950gal) low-mobility bulk tankers would distribute the fuel to rear combat areas. Here the fuel would be stored in tanks or smaller capacity tankers. The rear of the combat area would receive its fuel in medium-mobility 10,000ltr (2,200gal) tankers and from here 2,000ltr (440gal) fuel packs, on high-mobility trucks, would deliver to the fighting vehicles immediately behind the combat zone. Jerrycans would still remain for use when individual vehicles need to keep a supply of fuel on board. The plan was also to have the fuel packs demountable, to enable the trucks to carry out other duties.

Not surprisingly, there were Home Office regulations that governed the carriage of fuel. The Army was subject to them, but none of their vehicles had the mandatory double-pole wiring, battery master-switch, and metal fire screen between the load and the cab and the exhaust system.

With its high mobility, the Stalwart was looked on favourably by the Military Engineering and Experimental Establishment (MEXE) at Christchurch, Hampshire, who was to handle the project. In 1969 a Mk1 Stalwart was fitted with a single oval-section 2000ltr petrol tank. Soon after, four more Stalwarts were similarly fitted and given the designation 'Transportable Vehicle Refuelling Equipment' (TVRE). They were sent for trials with the BAOR who, considering the envisaged role of the Stalwart, would be the most suitable organization to assess the system. BAOR found bulk refuelling generally satisfactory, but the equipment itself would need to be

UBRE fitted to a Mk2 Stalwart. (REME Museum)

redesigned to make it suitable for the job. MEXE found that two rectangular-section tanks of aluminium would be the most suitable. In January 1972 the contract was put out to tender and Gloster-Saro was contracted to make them. The Stalwart needed little modification to make it meet the Home Office safety regulations. It was already fitted with a double-pole electrical system and the exhaust, rear mounted in its own box with a gauze cover, was considered safe. And there was already a double bulkhead behind the cab. The fuel would be dispensed through hoses pumped by a diesel-powered pump and jerrycans would be carried. The system would also have new name, Unit Bulk Refuelling Equipment – UBRE.

For the fifteen years from its introduction in 1975, UBRE worked well. There were some shortcomings, particularly with its installation on Stalwarts. If there was a mechanical breakdown, the tanks had to be unloaded before any fault in the engine compartment, however minor, could be fixed. And there was the danger of leaking fuel, which would drip onto the engine. A recommended course of action if this occurred was to lower the sides of vehicle to allow the fuel to drain off, but if a quantity had got into the hull often the most prudent course of action for the crew was to get out and run before it exploded!

WATER CANNON

In the early 1980s there was an element of civil unrest and some rioting in places like Brixton in London and Toxteth in Liverpool. Water cannon were in use by riot police in mainland Europe but, with the exception of Northern Ireland, not in the UK. In the riots police cars were being overturned, but a Stalwart with several tons of water on board could not be turned over that easily. Stalwart was nearing the end of its service life and there were quite few in storage, so an incentive came from Roland Andrews, then the Planning Manager at Alvis, to get the Home Office to have the vehicle adapted as a water cannon. The Home Office was very interested, but British Police Chiefs, who had never been keen on the use of water cannon, turned it down and the idea never went further than a suggestion.

Technical Specification – Mk2 (FV623)

Engine	
Type	One Rolls-Royce B81 Mk8B/2 in-line eight-cylinder petrol engine, cast-iron monobloc construction. Inlet-over-exhaust valves. Detachable iron cylinder head. Dry-sump lubrication
Bore	3½in (95.2mm)
Stroke	4½in (114.3mm)
Capacity	6,516cc
Power	220bhp at 4,000rpm
Torque (nett)	312lb ft at 2,400rpm
Compression ratio	6.5:1
Governed speed	3,750rpm
Ignition type	Coil 24v
Transmission	
Gearbox	Five-speed Alvis manual, synchromesh on second, third, fourth and top gears
Clutch	Borg and Beck twin 12in dry plate
Transfer box	Single range, forward and reverse, giving five forward and five reverse speeds, plus power take-off
Differential	Single, centrally mounted, 'No-Spin' device
Propeller shafts	Splined sleeve
Axles	Articulating shafts
Hub gearing	4.125:1 double epicyclic
Power take-off	Marine propulsion unit and winch/crane hydraulic pump
Drive in water	Two Dowty 12in diameter units driven from PTO on gearbox
Capacities	
Engine oil	3.5gal (15.9ltr)
Coolant	7gal (32ltr)
Gearbox oil	2.5gal (11.4ltr)
Fuel tank	95gal (405ltr)
Brakes	
Foot	Lockheed calliper-operated discs on all wheels
Hand	Mechanical, via transmission band type on front bevel box drums
Servo mechanism	Air servo
Steering	
System	Recirculating ball on front and centre axles
Servo mechanism	Hydraulic
Turning circle, left-right	50–60ft (15–18m)
Suspension	Independent on all six wheels, with unequal length wishbones and longitudinal torsion bars with sleeves giving 10in total travel. Damping by hydraulic shock absorbers and rebound dampers, two of each per front and rear wheel station, two shock absorbers and one rebound damper per centre wheel station
Wheels and Tyres	
Wheels	Divided disc, 10.00 × 20
Tyre size	14.00 × 20 fourteen ply

Technical Specification – Mk2 (FV623) (*cont.*)

Dimensions	
Length	20ft 10in (6.4m)
Height unladen	8ft 6in (2.6m)
Width	8ft 7in (2.62m)
Track	6ft 8 5/16in (2.04m)
Wheelbase	10ft (3m) overall (5ft, 5ft)
Ground clearance, unladen	1ft 7 3/8in (0.5m)
Weight, unladen, FV622	19,040lb (8,636kg)
Weight, unladen, FV623	23,184lb (10,515kg)
Fording Capability	To full flotation
Crew Capacity	Driver, plus up to two crew members in cab.
Performance	
Max road speed	43mph (67km/h)
Max speed cross-country	20mph (32km/h)
Max speed in water	5 knots
Max gradient	24 degrees
Max vertical obstacle	1ft 6in (0.5m)
Max approach angle	42 degrees
Max departure angle	29 degrees
Max trench crossing	5ft (1.5m)
Side unladen overturn	37 degrees
Range	450 miles (720km)
Load capacity	5 tons (5,080kg)
Electrical Equipment	24v DC for chassis, lighting and auxiliaries
Special Equipment	Fire extinguishing equipment around engine and fuel tank. Four towing eyes, one at each corner of vehicle, capable of towing a full load. Two towing eyes on side plates on side of vehicle, towing hook fitted at centre of rear skid plate
Maritime equipment	detachable rope or rubber fenders at each corner, navigation lighting to international maritime law.

Calm Amidst a Turbulent Sea – Alvis's Story from the Mid-1960s

During the 1950s and early 1960s, Alvis private car production was modest to say the least. Despite its hand-built quality, there were very few customers for the 3-litre TF, the traditional English gentleman's carriage. Accepting that Alvis's place as an independent car producer was no longer tenable, John Parkes spoke to Rover cars about the possibility of a merger. They took over Alvis in July 1965, trading share-for-share, and Parkes joined the board of Rover.

At this time, Rover's model line was a mixture. The Land Rover Series II had been in production since 1958, the big 3-litre saloon and coupé for as long, and the 2000 saloon since 1963. New car development costs were rising and, in late 1966, Rover welcomed an approach by Leyland who, since 1961, had owned Standard-Triumph. Rover, along with Alvis, became part of the Leyland group in December 1966.

The take-over did little to affect fighting vehicle production, but it was one of the factors that signalled the end of Alvis as a car maker. Any modern replacement for the 3-litre Alvis would be a competitor for Rover and Triumph models – the 2000 models of each marque already competed against each other. Just two years short of their half-century, Alvis announced they would cease car production from May 1967. It was a sad day at the 1966 Earls Court Motor Show. On the last day a party marked Alvis's departure, with every exhibitor turning up to bid them an emotional farewell.

In the spring of 1968, Leyland merged with British Motor Holdings, result of the recent amalgamation of BMC and Jaguar, to form the British Leyland Motor Corporation. The traumatic events that followed affected Alvis very little. Neither the internal politics that would affect model development in the new organization nor the fear of union action if plants were rationalized and jobs axed had any bearing on what was happening at Holyhead Road. They were concerned now with the production of fighting vehicles, none of which had any counterparts produced by either Leyland or BMH. In fact Alvis was now an odd man out within the corporation. One advantage came Alvis's way as a result of the merger. Meadows, who made the Stalwart gearbox, were taken over by Self-Change Gearboxes, the makers of the Wilson pre-selector gearbox used on the other three FV600s and, as a part of Jaguar (via Daimler), a part of British Motor Holdings. Alvis were merged with Self-Change Gearboxes as part of British Leyland Specialist Vehicles.

Only a couple of years after its creation BLMC began losing money heavily. In June 1975, in order to try and make a decent, profitable and stable organization out of the unwieldy mess, the Labour government of the day privatized it and renamed it British Leyland. The new Conservative government that came to power in 1979 under Margaret Thatcher was totally opposed to public ownership of any kind. They had to accept, however, that privatization for British Leyland would be a long way ahead. It had to be in a much better financial state before anyone would consider it a viable purchase. The head of the Chloride Group, South African-born Michael Edwardes, was brought in to try to make some sense of this huge mess that was costing the taxpayer dearly. The companies in the group that did not fit into the corporation's core business were sold off to raise cash. These included Coventry Climax, Prestcold Refrigeration and Alvis. United Scientific Instruments bought Alvis from BL for £27 million. Alvis later merged with GKN and moved from Coventry to Telford in Shropshire where the company continues to manufacture fighting vehicles.

Production Figures

Detailed records of Stalwart production exist and are, with minor exceptions, complete. Here is a breakdown compiled from data received from the Military Vehicle Section of the Alvis Owner Club.

Prototypes
There were fifteen Stalwart prototypes, PV1–PV15 inclusive. PV1–PV3 remained with Alvis. PV7–PV13 went into service with the British Army. Of the other prototypes, PV4 and PV5 went to Sweden, PV6 went to Italy, PV14 went to Germany and PV15 went to Berliet in France.

FV620
The Ministry of Defence ordered and received a total of 125 Mk1 FV620s. In addition, eight Mk1s went to the Swedish Coastal Artillery, one to Berliet. This makes a total of 135 Mk1 Stalwarts, not including STAL 56, which became the prototype Mk2.

FV622
The Ministry of Defence ordered 325 for the British Army, the Swedish coastal Artillery took eighteen, two went to the Bundeswehr in Germany and three went to Austria. Excluding STAL 56, this is a total of 348.

FV623, FV624
There were three FV623/624 prototypes. All production went to the British Army, which included 269 FV623s and sixty FV624s.

9 FV600s in Service

The FV600 series came into service at a crucial time in Britain's history. The defeat of Germany in the Second World War had brought many changes. As a result of having to depend on the USA to supply arms and men to conquer the Axis powers, Britain would no longer be a major world power, giving way to the USA and USSR.

And alongside Britain's commitment to the North Atlantic Treaty Organization, there was another story unfolding; the British Empire was being transformed into the Commonwealth. The dominions and dependencies of the British Empire, brought to Western-style standards of government, education and trade, sought independence. The transition would be traumatic for some African and Asian colonies. Following is an outline of some of the campaigns where the FV600 series would play an active part.

MALAYA

British troops were present in Malaya from the start of the emergency in 1948 until the country gained independence in 1960. The Malayan economy was based around rubber plantations and tin mines, under British control. Chinese and Indian labour had been brought in to work them. Malaya

This Saracen was on patrol in the Cameron Highlands in Malaya when the mountain road on which it was travelling gave way and it rolled down the mountainside. (REME Museum)

was over-run by the Japanese during the war and Malayan Chinese communists, under Chin Peng, aided the Malayan Peoples' Anti-Japanese Army, the MPAJA, which itself was supported by British Special Forces. When the Japanese surrendered, Chin Peng attempted to take power in Malaya, but the Malay people, constituting the majority of the population, did not want either Communists or the indigenous Chinese minority in power.

The Malayan Communist Party was recognized as legal, but its leaders launched an armed struggle, renaming their army the Malay Races Liberation Army (MRLA). Four fifths of Malaya is jungle, with a 6,000ft (1,830m) mountain range running north–south along its centre. The MRLA withdrew into the jungle to fight a guerrilla campaign whilst attempting to build political support. At first they had the upper hand, largely using surprise tactics. The police were understrength and under pressure. The only army presence was units of Gurkhas, which were under reorganization, and there was poor co-operation between them and the civil authorities.

In June 1948 Sir Henry Gurney, the High Commissioner for Malaya, declared a State of Emergency. To enforce it he brought the police up to strength, with both full-time officers and volunteer auxiliaries. In 1950 he requested Lt Gen (retd.) Harold Briggs to plan, co-ordinate and direct the anti-bandit operations of the police and fighting forces. Briggs' plan was to dominate the populated areas and build up a feeling of security. This would eventually encourage a flow of information on the Communists, enabling the security forces to seek and destroy the insurgents. Sir Henry established an integrated police and army organization to marshal the emergency and bring it under control.

Many of the Malay Chinese population were living in squatter villages, 'kampongs', on the edge of the jungle. Here was Chin Peng's bedrock of support, supplying his army with food. By the end of 1951 the great majority of these people were resettled in some 500 new villages, provided with clinics and schools, and giving them protection from intimidation.

The Communists continued their campaign, attacking prime targets like the rubber plantations and tin mines. The white civilian population were terrorized and the food convoys for the kampongs were attacked. The SAS, reformed as the Malaya Scouts, and the 21st UK Territorial SAS Regiment, reformed as 22nd SAS Regiment, were some of the early arrivals who sought out the guerrillas in the jungle and the mountains.

In October 1951 Sir Henry Gurney was murdered in an ambush. His replacement in January 1952 was General Sir Gerald Templer. He integrated the police and army activity and pursued a policy which stated that the whole population must be in the fight to combat communists. He maintained that the right way was not to pour more troops into the jungle, but to win the hearts and minds of the local people; to disrupt their daily lives as little as possible and to try to prevent at all costs any civilian casualties. On the positive side there should be involvement in the building of schools, roads, and the like, and medical assistance.

Sir Gerald Templer left Malaya in 1954, by which time the Communists were in retreat. The intelligence programme was achieving results, with many insurgents surrendering. In 1955 the Alliance Party under Tunku Abdul Rahman won a free election with a substantial majority. An amnesty was offered to MRLA but this was refused. Military assistance, including existing 22nd SAS and seventy-five men of the Parachute Regiment, who were trained in jungle warfare, was given to the new Malay government to fight off the remaining communist terrorists, driving them over the Thai border. Other regiments involved in the campaign were the 13/18th Royal Hussars, the 15/19th Hussars, the 11th Hussars, the 17th Gurkha Infantry, 12th Royal Lancers and the 21 UK Territorial Paratroop Regiment. Amongst those charged with keeping the Saracens and all the other motor transport running were the 221st Vehicle Maintenance Battalion. RASC. Malaya gained full independence in 1957 and the Army left entirely in 1960. In the whole campaign, 6,000 insurgents, 1,300 police and 500 soldiers lost their lives.

ADEN

Once a small part of the mighty Ottoman Empire, Aden is on the southwest of the Arabian peninsular. After the Great War, Britain was given a mandate to govern large tracts of the Middle East, which had been under Ottoman rule, making it a Crown colony. Barren land with a hot and humid climate, Aden's location was in an important oil-producing area and its natural harbour made it important strategically for Britain as a supply base for troops in the Indian Ocean and the Gulf.

In the 1950s, Aden Protectorate was a federation of small states. Aden town was the main conurbation, surrounded by Aden colony. The British mandate was to hold the federation together until such time as each constituent state was able to form a stable democratic government.

But democracy was a concept alien to the feudal tribesmen of the Protectorate. Nor were these people averse to occasional bandit raids on trading caravans journeying to Aden along the Dhala road. The rulers of the Yemen, Aden's neighbours, had a long-standing claim to Aden. Egypt's President Nasser provided the means for rebels under the chief of the Yemeni army, General Sallal, to overthrow their leader, Al Badr. Having survived the overthrow, Al Badr took refuge in the mountains and organized a fight back against Sallal, helped by SAS personnel.

Whilst the SAS men enjoyed considerable success against the regular Yemeni army, the pro-British rulers of the other Arab states were very concerned for their own security. And Aden and Yemeni opposition were backed by Egypt and thus associated with communism, as the Russians had given considerable assistance to Egypt's President Nasser after the Suez crisis. There were two organizations in the region. One was the National Liberation Front (NLF), which was communist. The Peoples Socialist Party was a political organization, but turned to terrorism as the Front for the Liberation of South Yemen (FLOSY). Conflict soon broke out between them. The situation escalated rapidly when, in December 1963, the British High Commissioner suffered a grenade attack where two people were killed and thirty others injured. A state of emergency was declared and in 1964 the nationalists began a guerrilla campaign against the British. Nationalists brought arms and men across the Yemeni border into mountainous Radfan territory. The Radfan tribes were violently independent. They resented any outside interference from the Aden Federation, actively harassing travellers and attacking government posts. The Federal government began a campaign in the Radfan and, after some hesitation, British Middle East command agreed to send British troops in support of the Federal Regular Army. In April 1964, 45 Commando, one company of the 3rd Parachute Regiment with engineers, artillery, armour and strike aircraft were sent to assist. The operation was not helped by scant information on the location of the tribesmen, but it achieved its objective of quelling the insurgents' activities for a time.

In November 1964 the NLF launched terrorist attacks on British servicemen and families, and government workers in Aden town. Based in safe houses in the Sheikh Othman, Crater and Maala areas, these attacks continued through the following year. The local people were scared to co-operate with British and Federal forces, making intelligence scarce. Unpopular house-to-house searches and cordon-and-search operations brought in some information.

Harold Wilson's Labour government decided in a White Paper in February 1966 that Britain would no longer need Aden as a base, rendering the whole British campaign impotent. In December both the NLF and FLOSY stepped up their terrorist campaign, inflicting high casualty figures among British troops. A UN anti-colonial faction witnessed orchestrated rioting Aden in April 1967 and, in June, 1 Para smashed the declaration by the NLF of the Sheikh Othman as a no-go area. A few days later the infamous Crater incident occurred, where a mutiny by Yemeni troops triggered a tragically chaotic scenario that resulted in the death of more than a dozen British troops. One of the

A British Army unit in convoy, with Saladin and Ferret armoured cars, followed by a Bedford RL three-tonner. (Tank Museum, Bovington)

The desert is an inhospitable place, as the crew of this FV603C Mk3 know. In this environment the suspension and cross-country capability of the Saracen was a great asset, and the reverse-flow cooling essential. (Tank Museum, Bovington)

attacked regiments, the Argyll and Sutherland highlanders, with 45 Commando, eventually retook the Crater and restored peace.

The British withdrew in November 1967, leaving Aden to govern itself. The NLF declared that they would take over. They rounded up and killed FLOSY members, unhindered by the British. Militarily the British were the more powerful and successful, but the changed political situation negated all military success. Some of the British Forces

REME Reminiscences

FV600s were in service with the British Army for around four decades and in that time it was the duty of the Corps of Royal Electrical and Mechanical Engineers (REME) to keep them operational. The vehicles were not without their problems and here is a selection of reminiscences by some ex-REME men.

Repairing the Stalwart

My first experience of the Stalwart was when I was posted to 4th Armoured Workshop in Detmold, Germany, in late 1972. This was part of a medium artillery unit and our battery had two Stalwarts for use as ammunition limbers. They were also used as fuel bowsers, carrying jerrycans to the self-propelled guns and HQ elements when on exercise. I remember on night exercise being called to a Stalwart that had broken down out on the ranges. The first thing we had to do was help unload all the jerrycans before we could lift the load-bay decks to get at the fault. This turned out to be leaking hydraulic slave cylinder on the accelerator linkage, a common fault. We fitted one and bled the system in fifteen minutes but then had to reload all those jerrycans.

For about a year at Detmold I worked on the Stalwart line carrying out engine and gearbox changes. Most of the work was clutch renewals for which we took the engine out. The clutch had two friction plates, which were not interchangeable. They could be fitted the wrong way round if you weren't careful. Unfortunately these mistakes would not reveal themselves until you tried to engage the gears after all had been refitted.

On my third tour of Northern Ireland I was part of the Forward Repair Group at Long Kesh workshop. We were responsible for the fitting of replacement engines, gearboxes and transfer boxes on Saracens throughout the province. We had two four-man teams, each headed by a sergeant, with a corporal (myself) as second in charge, a lance corporal driver and a craftsman. Each team had a Bedford RL fitted with a HIAB crane and a Land Rover. Where it was dangerous to drive, Crossmaglen for example, the new engine would be flown in by RAF Wessex helicopter and we would follow a few days later by small army helicopter to do the job. In all cases the unit's own REME fitter was responsible for carrying out the preparatory work, but this was not always possible. When changing the gearbox or transfer box we would remove the turret and top plate. To change a gearbox the steering unit had to be removed, which meant disconnecting the hydraulic pipes. The hydraulic fluid would mix with the soft paint and soon you would be plastered. Silver overalls, boots, the lot. After changing engines, we would put the fan belts on with a crowbar and flick the starter button, not recommended but much quicker than removing lock-wired bolts and splitting the adjustable pulleys.

To suspend tow a Saracen on its rear wheels for any distance you had to remove the sun gears from the rear reduction hubs. This was a time-consuming job and not the sort of thing you wanted to do on a Belfast street. It was rumoured that a lot of Saracens in the city had the gears permanently removed for speedy recovery and were, in effect, four-wheel drive only. Once the Saracen was recovered the gears had to be replaced, which, because the gears were epicyclic, meant that they had to be timed by lining up the five dot-marks. Get one dot mark out of line and the gear set would destroy itself in a couple of hundred yards.

Graham Howland

I joined my first unit, the 11th Hussars in Hohne in Germany in 1968. At that time they had just been fully equipped with Chieftain tanks and were getting new support vehicles, including Bedford Mks, FV432s, FV434s and Stalwarts. Initially the Stalwarts were Mk1s: I believe we had some Mk2s later in the year. As an HQ Squadron VMB one of my first jobs was to change the exhaust system on a Stalwart from a 2in to a 3in. The reason for the mod was that the 2in manifold and pipes were getting too hot and were cracking, as well as being a fire hazard. The mod should have taken about half a day, but being inexperienced I sheared a number of studs and took about two days to extract the broken ends. (No joke, working upside down!) It was then discovered that some manifold parts in the mod kit were the wrong pattern and the vehicle was on the shop floor for quite a while, waiting for replacements.

This exhaust modification must have been done on an 'as required' basis, as some were unmodified for a number of years. Back home in the UK we were on night exercise on Salisbury Plain. We were following the Stalwarts on convoy lights and we could see the exhausts miles away, which were glowing cherry red!

Some Stalwarts were used to refuel the Centurions from jerrycans. This was not a good idea in retrospect as, around 1970, one of the Mk1s, (possibly 23 EK 23 or 24 EK 24), which had split decks, caught fire and was completely burned out. Some of the jerrycans were found several hundred yards away. After that, only Mk2s with a one-piece deck were used for carrying fuel.

Steve Gray

Saracen Repairs

When I first went to BAOR in 1966, the first job I did on a Saracen was to carry out a top overhaul. The alloy head had suffered gas erosion between two cylinders and therefore required replacement. I had never worked on a B80 before and, without any supervision, got on with the job. After removing all the nuts on the cylinder head (I believe that there were forty-nine of them), the head would still not come off. The next step was to attach the overhead crane to the head and proceeded to lift. It still would not come off and the front wheels of the Saracen started to lift off the ground. Some bright spark then asked if I had removed the nut that was inside the exhaust port. We let the crane down and removed the nut, but the head would still not come off. Up went the crane again, the front wheels came off the ground, and this time a crow bar was used to free the head. We eventually worked it up the forty-nine cylinder-head studs, which seemed about a foot long. The removal was a problem because the alloy cylinder-head had corroded so badly on the head studs. I can remember squatting on top of the front wings cleaning all the alloy corrosion off the head studs with emery cloth. It took hours, and I then painted them with rust-preventing paint. After waiting many weeks the new cylinder head turned up, and I am sure that it was a cast-iron one. I remember dropping one of the exhaust-valve spring collets down into the sump. Much to my relief it came out when I drained the oil, or out would have to come the engine.

Trevor Piper

From 1961 until 1965 I was serving as a gun fitter in the LAD of 40 Field Regiment Royal Artillery in Munster, West Germany. To support our two batteries of 25pdrs and one battery of 5.5-inch guns we were equipped with FV610 Saracen Armoured Command Post vehicles, two per battery, and HQ vehicles. As a gun fitter I was not involved in the repair of these vehicles, but being very tall I had certain abilities that were in great demand by the vehicle mechanics. I was the only member of the LAD that could reach the floor of the engine compartment with my arm when lying on top of the engine. Whilst carrying out repairs the VMs were always dropping their spanners and after struggling to retrieve them with bits of wire and the like, they would send for me. If a more major repair was involved and the front armour plate was removed, VMs from all over the shop would appear to claim any tools dropped during earlier work on the vehicle.

After leaving the army I served for several years in the TA, serving with C Squadron, the Royal Yeomanry, stationed in Croydon. This was from 1971 until 1973. This was the period when the troubles in Northern Ireland were at their most violent and we would often arrive at the drill hall on training nights only to find several of the Saracens had been commandeered and sent to Belfast. When they returned they were in quite a state; bent, battered, covered in various colours of paint and with bits and pieces missing. On one occasion that this happened we were preparing for the Lord Mayor's show and it caused us an awful lot of hard work to get the vehicles ready for the parade.

M.J. Tanner

REME Reminiscences (*cont.*)

The Kineton Salamander

When I was a Staff Sergeant Artificer Vehicles in NI in early 1973, I was called to look at the ex-Kineton Salamander at Girwood Park, Belfast. The beast was being used to spray water on riots to break up the gatherings. It had lost reverse gear, essential for reversing out of the then very frequent riots in the city. It was recovered to the Royal Navy Aircraft Yard next to Harland and Wolff's shipyard in Belfast where our workshop was located. The reverse gear is in the transfer box, which just happens to be right in the middle of the vehicle. Working on Stalwart, Saladin and Saracen was a 'complete doddle' compared with this particular beast. It was a real pig and appeared to be made up of various bits. There were no workshop manuals for it. It did not have the split-coupling centre-wheel stations, which meant that they also had to be removed to get the transfer gearbox out. The rear of the vehicle had to be removed, then the radiators and fans to get at the engine. The water tank was welded on (I suspect after all the machinery had been installed), so there was no top access to the machinery like the Stalwart. Needless to say, the tank was porous and rusty water was dripping everywhere into the engine compartment. You had to crawl in beside the engine to undo all the bell-housing bolts to the gearbox, exhaust and electrical connections. Space was extremely tight. After we had improvised a 12ft-long lifting beam, we got the engine out through the hole in the back of the vehicle. We then had to crawl back in to disconnect the epicyclic gearbox, which had to come out the same way before you could get at the transfer box. When we had it out on the workshop floor and took the side off, the selectors were all broken, and some of the metal had damaged the gearwheels.

Fire appliances in NI were top priority in those days and the RAF in Germany held the only spare transfer box. They duly flew it in that night, but we found that the casing was different and the power take-off was in a different place. After working non-stop for nearly twenty-four hours to get the beast in pieces in cold wet conditions, you only have to imagine how impressed we were. Being REME, we sat down for another cup of tea to review the way forward and, ever mindful of the pressure to fix the beast, we took all of the internals out of the new transfer box and fitted them into the old transfer box casing, improvising as necessary. This took a further six hours and then we had to put the whole lot back into the Salamander again. By the time we waved goodbye to it, we had been going nearly forty-eight hours – knackered is an understatement. But we must have got it right, as we never thankfully saw the thing again. I can honestly say that it is the most difficult vehicle that I ever worked on in thirty-eight years. We did have some good fun with it, charging along the other workshop located further down the airfield from us spraying them with water. (They got us back a few days later when they had an ordinary fire engine in for repair.)

Trevor Piper

Driving the FV600s

I drove a Stalwart a few times. You had to remember not to lift your foot off the throttle or the No-Spin diff banged in and out of mesh, causing the vehicle to waddle around the bend in an alarming fashion. The unusual gearchange pattern caused a lot of confusion until you got used to it.

I enjoyed driving the Saracens when I had the chance. With power steering and the Wilson pre-selector box they were easy to drive and the sound of that straight eight and the howl of the cooling fans was something to savour. I had several very enjoyable afternoons on the perimeter track of Long Kesh airfield. A big problem with the FV600 series was transmission wind-up. A means of relieving the stress was to drive the vehicle up and down the kerb every few miles. With hindsight I quite like the FV600 series. They were certainly different!

Graham Howland

Around this time (1970) the regiment went to Marchwood and loaded onto LSLs to do a beach landing at Lulworth. As our MT Troop had never floated their Stollies they persuaded the crew to let them drive into the water (tied up in harbour of course) out of the loading deck. The ramp was lowered and the troop drove down and took to the water as if it was an everyday occurrence, did a circuit of the harbour and drove back onto the deck again, much to everyone's amusement (or amazement in some cases!). I have to say that this was the only time I ever saw Stalwarts swimming. One of the LAD corporals, Nobby Clarke, who had been with the trials team some years before, said the trials version he remembered performed much better, in and out of the water, as it had a six-cylinder French diesel engine instead of the B81.

Around 1971 the well-known CVJ problems became common and all the wheel stations had lines painted across the hubs to show up any defective ones. I do recall a hair-raising episode when I was called out one evening to fix a Stalwart that had broken down and ended up being towed back to Tidworth by one of the others. Despite my plea for the driver to 'take it slowly' as there was no power steering or braking, he shot off at great speed and it was all I could do to control the casualty. It worked wonders for my arm and leg muscles!

Around 1970 or 1971, legislation meant that all drivers of six-wheeled vehicles had to pass the new HGV test so, as the only six-wheelers we had were Stalwarts, that's what we took our tests in. This was no problem for the majority, who had been driving them for a while but a few, including the EME, just jumped in for the test with no chance to get used to the vehicle, with predictable results. I recall the instructor, who was standing on the passenger seat, almost catapulted out of the hatch when it came to an emergency stop. They did have effective brakes!

I still have a great affection for Stalwarts. They were excellent vehicles and a bit of investment in a better engine could have seen them given a new lease of life instead of being withdrawn when they were.

Steve Gray

Troops who had to ride in the Saracen often complained of seasickness and disorientation when travelling across country. Anyone who has had to follow tanks across Hohne, Soltau and Munsterlager ranges in Germany, in wheeled vehicles will agree that it is not the most pleasant experience.

M.J. Tanner

who served in Aden were the RAF Regiment, 4th Parachute Regiment, 45 Commando, the Lancashire Regiment, the Royal Northumberland Fusiliers, the Argyll and Sutherland Highlanders and the South Staffordshire Regiment.

BORNEO

British Borneo was made up of three territories – Sarawak, Brunei and North Borneo. A mountain range created a natural divide between them on the northern side and the remainder of island. The Malayan prime minister, Tunku Abdul Rahman, wanted these three territories in his new Malaysian Federation, which Britain favoured, but President Sukarno of Indonesia wanted the territories as part of a greater Indonesia. On 8 December 1962 the Sultanate of Brunei suffered a revolt, led by a Sukarno sympathizer, A.M. Azahari, with forces led by Yassin Effendi. Their plan was to capture guns from police stations, seize Brunei's oilfields and capture the Sultan. The rebellion started successfully, but the police knew of the plan in advance and the rebels failed to get into the Sultan's palace. Two companies of Gurkhas were sent from Singapore, crushing the rebellion within days.

But Sukarno wanted revenge and launched a raid by 'volunteers' across the border from Borneo who attacked Tebedu police station. A British campaign to stop Sukarno began from 19 December 1962 across the 970mile (1,500km) mountainous land border and 1,500mile (2,400km) coastline. A small police force and five battalions of British troops used the same tactics as were used in Malaya. These were good intelligence and control of the jungle by: denying insurgents access to supplies; winning the hearts and minds of the people; keeping soldiers and police in villages to protect people; and supplying medical and agricultural help. Local tribesmen formed the basis of an irregular force, the Border Scouts. The use of helicopters, hovercraft and small boats was a great asset in supplying remote jungle areas and in dropping SAS into jungle to fight guerrillas.

This Saracen was in service until the late 1990s with the Hong Kong Police. (Tank Museum, Bovington)

Sukarno halted his campaign and tried a third method of sending in Indonesian regular soldiers. But he faced a British-led Commonwealth force of thirteen infantry battalions, two engineers regiments, two artillery regiments, an SAS battalion, helicopters, aircraft and small naval vessels. The British took the initiative by moving further into the jungle, stationing artillery along whole border and using the SAS to infiltrate further into forward positions. Sukarno was now denied a foothold in the area. He was deposed in March 1966 by President Suharto, who signed a peace treaty with the new federation of Malaysia. The Borneo campaign was an example of good co-operation between the British Army, the RAF and the Royal Navy, and local police.

THE COLD WAR – BRITISH TROOPS IN GERMANY

A huge threat to the rule of democracy and to world stability came from the USSR. Russia had suffered the most terrible losses during the German invasion, launched in late 1940. Millions died in combat, often hand to hand in the streets of cities like Stalingrad (now Volgograd), in what Russians call the Great Patriotic War. The huge open spaces of Russia are no natural defence to any invader, whether Ghengis Khan coming from the east, or Napoleon or Hitler driving in from the west. As a protection for their vulnerable western borders, the Russian leader, Josef Stalin, seized the countries they had liberated from the Nazis – Poland,

A Stalwart Mk2 Logistics vehicle with an Atlas crane, stationed in Germany. (REME Museum)

Czechoslovakia, Hungary, Romania, the Baltic States and, most crucially, the eastern third of Germany as satellites of the Communist regime. These would be a natural geographical buffer.

Western Germany was divided amongst the allies, France occupying two southwestern zones, the USA the bulk of the central eastern part and Britain the northern third. Berlin, the capital of both the Kaiser's Second and Hitler's Third Reich, was in the heart of the new communist German Democratic Republic, and was divided like the rest of Germany. The Russians effectively controlled the eastern half and the western half was divided between the Americans, the French and the British. Behind what Winston Churchill called the Iron Curtain, the USSR built up huge armies and stocks of conventional and nuclear weapons to ward off any threat of invasion. To counter this, NATO would station land and air forces in Germany. In 1961, as a response to the steady exodus of Germans to the west through Berlin, the East German government built a wall across the city. This was to symbolize, in concrete terms, the division in a far starker way than even Churchill's epithet 'Iron Curtain' and polarized the two sides even further.

Although the Hungarian uprising in 1956 and the Czech Revolution of 1967 were brutally crushed by Russia, the Cold War never erupted into full-scale combat across Central Europe as feared. In 1987 the Soviet Union received a fatal blow when the Berlin Wall was destroyed with as little physical opposition as when it was built. The Cold War was all but over, and many NATO bases would be closed.

SALADINS AND SARACENS WITH THE RAF

As well as Salamanders and Stalwarts, the RAF would, for a short period of time, use Saladins and Saracens. They were in service with the RAF Regiment, a force formed during the Second World War to relieve the British Army of the duty of guarding RAF stations. As told in Chapter 1, the RAF had used armoured cars during the 1920s. No. 1 Armoured Car Company (ACC) was formed at Heliopolis in December 1921. It was incorporated into the RAF Regiment as 2701 Squadron in

October 1946, although disbanded in January 1948. It reappeared in the early 1960s as No. 1 Field Squadron, charged with the role of low-level air defence. In 1970 it moved to Laarbruch in Germany, from where Jaguars of No. 2 Squadron and Buccaneers of No. 16 Squadron were flown. Situated on the Dutch border, Laarbruch was of high strategic importance. In 1974 No. 1 Field Squadron's role changed once more, becoming one of the new light armoured RAF regiment squadrons that were due to be equipped with the new CVR(T) tracked vehicles.

A Saracen crew of RAF Regiment No. 1 Field Squadron stationed at Laarbruch take a breather. (Nigel Sheldon)

However, No. 1 Field Squadron was not to receive the new vehicles immediately. They were loaned a number of FV600s from the BAOR as an interim measure. There would be three Saladins, which were sent to Laarbruch in 1978, supported by the RAF's own Ferret armoured cars. From 1981, 'A' Flight would operate Saracens. Also on strength were a number of Land Rovers. Unlike the two Stalwart Reef Rescue Vehicles, the FV600s would retain their Army registration marks.

When the new Sultan tracked armoured command vehicle was introduced from 1981, the three Saladins and one Saracen were then moved to RAF Brüggen until 1982, the remaining Saracens either being put into store or used by 50 Field Squadron Royal Engineers for runway and end of runway repair. One or two were also kept by 2 Squadron for their Explosive Ordnance and Demolition teams, alongside the their new Scimitar armoured reconnaissance vehicles and Spartan APCs, until at least 1990. Also on loan from the BAOR, a single Saracen was posted to Gütersloh, Germany, halfway between Hanover and Dortmund, where Nos 3 and 4 Squadrons were flying Harriers.

Two Saracens, one with RFC, were converted to a mine exploder role. They were transferred to HQ Air Forces, Gulf, in February 1970 and deployed at RAF Salalah, Aden. Two Saladins, one from Hong Kong and another from the Queens Dragoon Guards, both via Central Vehicle Depot, Ludgershall, were transferred to 721 Signals Unit, RAF, in September 1976. Like the vehicles at the RAF stations in Germany, these all retained the Army registration marks. CVR (T) delivery to the RAF Regiment began in 1981. They would replace the FV600s and Ferrets, which were kept in storage until as late as 1995 before they were sold off.

NORTHERN IRELAND

For almost a thousand years Britain claimed sovereignty over Ireland and throughout that time there were attempts to establish Irish independence. The first move towards that had been the establishment in 1921 of the controversial Irish Free State, a self-governing Dominion within the British Empire. But the island was divided: Protestant Unionists in the north insisted that six of the counties of Ulster remained under British rule. The Republic of Ireland was created as a totally independent state in 1949, but Northern Ireland remained a part of the United Kingdom. Further attempts by the Irish Republican Army, who had played a crucial role in the move towards independence, failed to create a united Ireland.

The cages on this Saracen were to nullify the effects of Soviet-made RPG-7 rockets, which were in the hands of Irish terrorists. (REME Museum)

A Mk3 Saracen APC with interior security modifications, including grilles over the periscopes and lights, and a front 'bullbar' to move rioters. (REME Museum)

A Saracen with experimental water cannon equipment, photographed at Chertsey. (REME Museum)

Catholics in the north were the victims of 'blatant discrimination', having the highest unemployment and the worst housing. In these communities, especially in the cities of Belfast and Londonderry, was the bedrock support of republicanism. But moves were afoot in Westminster and in the Northern Irish parliament at Stormont Castle to try and redress the balance. This was resisted by the Protestant Unionists and in 1968 a civil rights march in Londonderry to try and secure good housing for Catholics was broken up by the police. In retaliation more-militant factions began a campaign of bombing public utilities.

In 1969 two days of rioting by Catholics broke out after a Protestant march in Londonderry's Bogside. Later that year troops were sent in to protect Catholics from Protestant riots in Belfast's Shankhill district. But later, Catholic civilians were to die during riots. The British Army were caught in the middle of three decades of political wrangling, and a terrorist conflict between republicans on one side and those loyal to the Crown on the other.

Working alongside the Royal Ulster Constabulary, the Army's tasks were in essence twofold. One was to defeat the terrorist activities of bombing and killing by both undercover work and by high levels of security in cities and the countryside. The other was to repress the rioting that took place in the streets of Belfast and Londonderry.

In order to carry out this task, numbers of ageing Saracen APCs were pulled out of Territorial Army barracks around Britain and put to use on the streets and in the countryside. These vehicles were chosen for a quite specific political reason. It had only been a few short years since the Russians sent tanks into Prague to quell the Czechoslovakian President Alexander Dubcek's attempt at reform. There was international outrage. The British Army's new APC was the FV432, which as we have seen was a tracked vehicle. The last thing the British government wanted to see was a newspaper headline declaring 'Tanks on Belfast Streets'.

Some of the Saracens sent to Northern Ireland were new. They were part of an export order for

This Mk1 Saracen has a more dignified retirement than those used as hard targets. It is used as a load in the tests of a Scammell EKA recovery in the mid-1980s. The Scammell was not chosen and a Foden selected instead. (REME Museum)

Libya, cancelled when Colonel Qaddafi seized power. These were fitted with RFC and had their desert camouflage quickly sprayed over with green paint. Water cannon was tried as a means of controlling riots. The Army's Salamander fire tender was transferred to Northern Ireland and converted. Elaborate equipment was designed for installation in a Saracen. This would deliver water in two ways: one as a lower pressure jet to simply soak groups of rioters and the other as a single 'slug' of high pressure to take out an individual without causing permanent injury. Some Saracens were fitted out with wire cages to protect them from attacks from Soviet-made RPG-7 rockets that were being supplied to the Provisional IRA. Also, additional external equipment was fitted that included large 'nudge bars' to enable the vehicles' drivers to push rioters at low speed. But the one feature of the Saracen that made it perform well cross-country, its six-wheel configuration, was to be its downfall in Northern Ireland. Rioters found it easy to immobilize a Saracen by rolling an aluminium beer keg under the wheels. This would jam between the front and centre wheels. The Army replaced the Saracens with the four-wheeled FV1611 Humber 'Pig' which resolved this partiucular problem.

DISPOSAL

There is little room for nostalgia when it conflicts with service requirements. The FV600s were well respected and gave good service but, although the Saracen and Stalwart ran on for longer than expected, eventually they went the way of all obsolete vehicles. After service in the Territorial Army, most were sold off to approved distributors. In Germany they were driven to the Army's disposal depot at Recklinhausen. Other FV600s, notably the Saracens, met an ignominious end as hard targets for tank and armoured car regiments and the RAF. Some were used as towed vehicles for the training of REME recovery crews and a few remain as gate guards at some Army barracks. A few have been preserved, and some of these are mentioned in the following chapter.

10 FV600s in Preservation

Some Stalwarts in civilian life have been modified to suit their owners' particular needs. This conversion is a motor home. (Terry Welsh)

The most commonly preserved FV600 is the Stalwart, mainly because it was the last in service and sold out as the interest in vehicle preservation in all fields was growing. Some have been restored to their original specification either as Mk1s or Mk2s, whilst others have been modified to suit their owner's preferences. One particular vehicle was painted pink for a Boots the Chemist commercial and later sold on. The buyer, who owns other Stalwarts, decided to keep the colour. Saracens are the second most commonly preserved of the family. Because of their long service life they too were sold off in time to coincide with the preservation boom.

Most Saracens around today are Mk2s, including an ACV and there are a smaller number of Mk1s. The Tank Museum has an FV604 on display with its canvas extension set up. Many are kept as 'gate guards' at Army camps, particularly Territorial

One of the pleasant surprises one encounters in the vehicle preservation movement is that the most surprising vehicles turn up in the most unexpected times. This is an RAF FV653 Driver Training Vehicle, offered for sale from a field in 1999. (Anthony Kendrick)

Army barracks as the TA were the last to have them.

Some Salamanders are in preservation – two are at Headcorn, Kent and are owned privately. There is one at Norwich airport and another is at the RAF Museum in Hendon. One example in the Fire Museum at Manston, Kent, was destined for preservation from the time it was withdrawn from service. Whilst it was in the charge of RAF Maintenance

This remarkable vehicle is actually a Salamander, converted to private off-road competition use. It is said to be a very hard vehicle to beat in its class. (Terry Welsh)

Command, a request was made for it to be saved for the Museum at Catterick. It did not go there, but was downgraded for instructional assembly at RAF Wyton. Eventually it found its way to Manston where it can be seen, like the whole museum, by appointment. The RAF Fire Services Trust has two, one restored and another undergoing restoration at the Bentley Wildfowl Trust, Sussex. One particular vehicle has had a new body fitted and the owner uses it in off-road competitions.

Although the Saladin was the most numerous of the FV600 family, most went to overseas buyers, the British Army buying just 248. It is now a very rare animal and a good example can fetch a sum in sterling approaching five figures. They also mount a big gun, which itself adds to the vehicle's desirability. The first of the Crossley prototypes is in the Tank Museum in Bovington and an example of the Alvis production run is at Bletchley Park. Another Saladin has been bought for a museum in Germany to represent the vehicles used by the Bundesgrenzschutz. A few examples survive as gate guards.

MUSEUMS

The difficulties facing any museum are having sufficient space to display all it has and finding funds for both renovation and display. The Tank Museum is no exception, with more FV600s in storage than can be shown. The REME Museum of Technology is in a similar predicament, with just one Stalwart, an FV624 naturally, on display in the Prince Philip Hall. But amongst their huge collec-

Museums often rely on volunteer help to bring their exhibits up to a standard suitable for display. This Saracen, which has its reverse flow cooling bodywork removed, is undergoing such renovation. (Bill Munro)

tion of other vehicles, they have several Stollies, Saracens (including a Royal Armoured Corps converted FV603B Signals vehicle) and Saladins in storage, all awaiting renovation. Thankfully both museums, as well as many other such establishments, have superbly kept libraries with documents on all types of military vehicle, available for inspection by appointment by the serious researcher.

USING AND ENJOYING PRESERVED FV600s

All four members of the FV600 family would qualify for entry in any of the military vehicle shows held all over the world. Because of its rarity one would be extremely lucky to see a Salamander and the fact is that, like other FV600s and armoured vehicles in general, it is not an ideal vehicle to drive on public roads. The most common sight would be Stalwarts in either Mk1 or Mk2 forms, or occasionally limber or REME versions.

As expected, Saracens are the next most numerous to be seen at shows, in Mk1 or Mk2 APC form. One might occasionally find an ACV. The FV610 is an extremely rare vehicle and one would be very lucky to see one. Saladins, as explained, are also a rare sight – in fact you now are more likely to see rare American, German or Soviet vehicles than an example of one of the finest armoured cars that Britain produced.

Many big military vehicle shows are held in Britain throughout the summer season and there are also runs to continental Europe, especially to

This Mk1 Stalwart had been subject to alterations during its Army service, but now has been restored to its original form. It is pictured here driving to the main arena of the War and Peace Show. (Bill Munro)

Seen without a turret, this APC is part of a private museum collection. It served with the BAOR, first with the 15/19 Hussars and later with 667 Squadron Army Air Corps, and is displayed in the markings of the Royal Anglian Regiment. It had been fitted with RFC and still retains the 'beehives'. (Bill Munro)

Bethune in Northern France and to Normandy for D-Day commemorations. The biggest show in Britain is the War and Peace Show held at the Hop Farm at Beltring, in north Kent, run by the Invicta Military Vehicle Preservation Society – the IMPS. 'Beltring', as it is always known amongst its regulars, is held in mid-July and attracts literally thousands of vehicles, ranging in age from Great War veterans to the latest available, such as earlier models of the American Humvee dating from the early 1980s. Other events include the Military Vehicle Trust shows at Berkeley Castle, Gloucestershire, and Denmead, Hampshire.

At all of these shows one can see the vehicles on static display, either on their own or as part of a diorama including the related equipment. If there is a main arena in the showground there will be re-enactments. These are more than likely to represent either Second World War or Vietnam action. Whilst we have yet to see such displays featuring the theatres of war in which FV600s were involved, plans are in hand to present a NATO exercise showing the role of the Stalwart in supporting Abbot self-propelled guns and other armour.

The Stalwart has a dedicated following, especially within the Alvis Owner Club Military Vehicle Section. Whilst the club caters for all Alvis fighting vehicles, the 'Stolly' is the most common. Members take every opportunity they can to swim their vehicles, whether in a lake or a river, and club weekend trips will aim to arrange this wherever possible. Just like any other vehicle enthusiasts' club, the Alvis Owner Club's Military Vehicle Section members

A line up of Stalwarts on an Alvis Owner Club Military Vehicle Section trip to the Lake District. Parked outside a Penrith pub the vehicles are, from the left, an early FV622, an FV620, a late FV622 and an FV623. All are in excellent order and all swim. (Anthony Kendrick)

Two Stalwarts, an FV620 (left) and an FV623 swimming on Ullswater. (Anthony Kendrick)

can source spare parts, discuss technical problems and swap yarns about the various experiences they have had with their vehicles. Stolly owners can tell some pretty hairy stories, not least those of an aquatic nature!

Restoring an FV600, like any big military vehicle, is not a small job. Whilst they are not excessively expensive to buy, they are big and, as such, need a large storage space and heavy lifting equipment is necessary if an engine removal has to be undertaken. And spare parts are becoming scarce. Military vehicle spare parts dealers do hold some stocks, but these are dwindling and none are currently being remanufactured. Now the main recourse is to cannibalize other vehicles, which is in some way a shame as the donor vehicles themselves may well be in a restorable condition.

But wherever you see an FV600, you will find it, like all military vehicles, in the hands of a genuine enthusiast. Owners will be happy to discuss their pride and joy with you. If you are an ex-serviceman or woman who has had experience with an FV600, the owners will be very pleased to listen to your stories. If you are not ex-service but an interested spectator, please be willing to listen and learn and to respect the considerable effort these vehicles' owners put in to keep these truly fine examples of British craftsmanship in running order.

Glossary

AFDFS	Armed Forces Defence Fire Service
ACP	Armoured Command Post (Royal Artillery)
ACV	Armoured Command Vehicle
ACRT	Aircraft Crash Rescue Truck
AFV	Armoured Fighting Vehicle
AP	Armour Piercing
APC	Armoured Personnel Carrier
BAOR	British Army of the Rhine
BSF	British Standard Fine (thread size)
CVJ	Constant Velocity Joint
CVR(T)	Combat Reconnaissance Vehicle (tracked)
DP	Dual Purpose (RAF fire crash tender)
DSRD	Directorate of Supply, Research and Development
DTD	Department of Tank Design
D & D	Design and Development
D & M	Design and Modification
FACE	Field Artillery Computer Equipment
FARELF	Far Eastern Land Forces
FEAF	Far East Air Force
FVDD	Fighting Vehicle Design Department
FVRE	Fighting Vehicles Research Establishment
FVRDE	Fighting Vehicles Research and Development Establishment
FMC	Food Machinery and Chemical Corporation
HE	High explosive
HMLC	High Mobility Load Carrier
HV	High Velocity
MEAF	Middle East Air Force
MELF	Middle East Land Forces
MFV	Major Foam Vehicle
MoD	Ministry of Defence
MoS	Ministry of Supply
MPAJA	Malayan Peoples' Anti-Japanese Army
MRLA	Malay Races Liberation Army
MVEE	Military Vehicles and Engineering Establishment

NATO	North Atlantic Treaty Organization
OTAC	Ordnance Tank-Automotive Command
PTO	Power take-off
RAC	Royal Armoured Corps
RAF	Royal Air Force
RAMC	Royal Army Medical Corps
RAOC	Royal Army Ordnance Corps
RASC	Royal Army Service Corps
RARDE	Royal Armament Research and Development Establishment
RCAF	Royal Canadian Air Force
RCYAF	Royal Ceylon Air Force
(C) REME	(Corps of) Royal Electrical and Mechanical Engineers
RFC	Reverse flow cooling, Royal Flying Corps
RHA	Royal Horse Artillery
ROF	Royal Ordnance Factory
RUC	Royal Ulster Constabulary
SAAF	South African Air Force
SAE	Society of Automobile Engineers
SAS	Special Air Service
UNF	Unified National (fine) (thread size)
VHF	Very high frequency
WD	War Department
WO	War Office
WT	Wireless Transmitter

Index